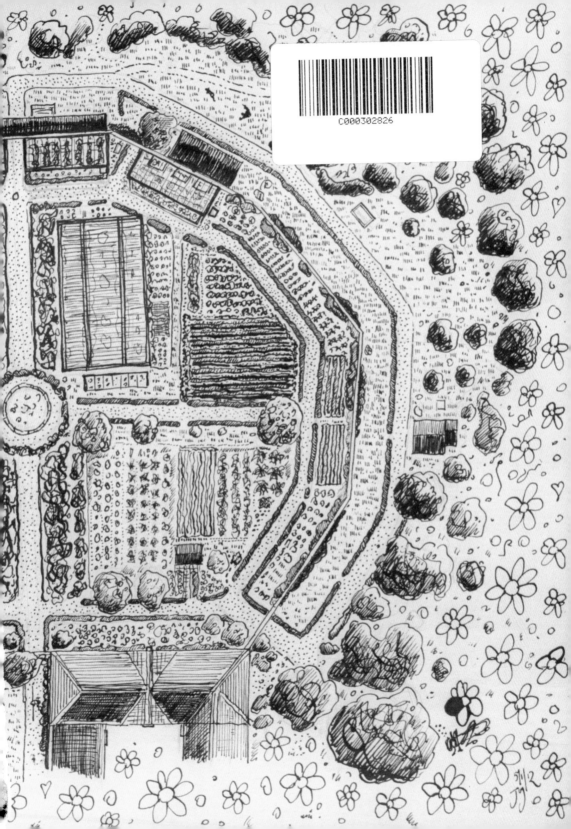

AN ARTIST IN THE GARDEN

A YEAR IN A SUFFOLK WALLED GARDEN

AN
ARTIST
IN THE
GARDEN

A YEAR IN A SUFFOLK WALLED GARDEN

TESSA NEWCOMB
JASON GATHORNE-HARDY

FOREWORD BY RONALD BLYTHE

FULL CIRCLE EDITIONS

Contents

Left: The flower house

Foreword

TWO ARTISTS in fact, one with her moth's wing
sentences and painterly response to what she saw within these tall walls,
the other with an inherited comprehension of their purpose allied to a
deep love of the modest countryside surrounding them. They make a
perfect partnership. Together they have created a very special East
Anglian book. Although frequently imaginative, even visionary, it is
grounded in toil – the never-ending labour of the seasons. Suffolk is full
of walled gardens, great and small. They shelter behind ancient streets
and parish churches, and make existence comfortable in coastal towns.
But the walled garden of a Georgian country house is not so much a
convenience as a realm. *An Artist in the Garden* admits the reader to this
realm and its unique wonders, its purpose and its climate. Has there
ever been a more complete inventory of what a classic walled garden
contains? These lists alone, made with such understanding and
affection, are a little history in themselves.

The walled garden of Glemham House might be described as a kind
of horticultural theatre with its backdrops of climbers, enclosed
atmosphere and dramatic annual productions, but it is also a
contemplative place, a combined inside and outside realm which
nourishes the spirit as well as the body. Purely practical in its origin, two
centuries of roses, cut grass and edible plants have taken it into the
realm of meditation and imagination. Which is what Tessa Newcomb
and Jason Gathorne-Hardy have recognised. A celebrated 19th century
German gardener stood and looked at his garden for an hour before he so
much as picked up his spade or pulled a weed. This every day. Although
filled with every kind of work, old and new, and carrying a well-told
burden of necessary local history, this is essentially a contemplative

story of the happiness to be found in the growing of what we eat. Country houses like Glemham were built to feed communities as much as families. With her remarkable knowledge of food, Caroline Cranbrook might be said to have taken the walled garden produce out into the community at large, and into all our lives. Her recipes, with those of other contributors, follow the year in this book, just as they would have followed the walled garden months, and with exciting seasonal tastes.

Each of us, wherever we come from and whenever we exist, 'possess' a certain place on our own terms, and surrounding this walled garden we have the story of its setting, the Alde Valley. It is a tale told from scratch, or from its creation in pre-history, and through all the social and agricultural change since it was built. Its site, native flora, domestic cultivation and present inspiration – for as this excellent account proves it has taken on a thrilling new life – are given both their intellectual and romantic dues. One way or another the entire modern history of the parish might be said to have been filtered through this productive enclosure. Many names are given. They make grateful biographies. The botanist poet George Crabbe was rector here. Both Jason's father and grandfather were/are remarkable naturalists here, and this book makes Jason a true successor in the field. Taking a walled garden as a symbol of how we should all attempt to live in the countryside, he and Tessa show how many of its tasks and rewards, its dreams and seasons can exist where ever we put in a spade. Hard graft and philosophy, horticulture and kitchen skills, doing nothing and being 'on the goo', as they say in Suffolk, all these things come together in this beautiful book. A little river encompasses them, a knowledgeable hand reveals them in language and pictures. It makes a fascinating addition to rural literature and is in a class of its own.

Ronald Blythe

Introduction

"In the ensuing Gipping Glaciation ice again advanced into East Anglia but this time from a more northerly direction across north-west Norfolk down into Suffolk… In the high-lying plateau areas of mid-Norfolk and mid-Suffolk, Gipping ice passed over the remnants of the Lowestoft Till with progressive incorporation of its debris… Where, as is usually the case, the outwash is non-calcareous, it has given rise to brown earths of low base status, podzolic brown earths and humus podzols. These are specially characteristic of the Cromer Ridge and some of the outwash areas between it and Norwich, and of the east Suffolk heaths."

R M S Perrin, East Anglian Forests, Forestry Commission

A FEW HUNDRED THOUSAND years ago the North Sea was no more than a large bay on the north shores of Europe. It was a cold landscape, across which large mammals and palaeolithic humans migrated to and fro. As ice caps melted and sea levels rose, this land bridge was slowly inundated, leaving a more familiar outline to the land masses on either side. There have been minor ice ages and retreats since, but none so large as the Gipping Glaciation. The shape of coastlines has continued to shift and alter, but more by the endless motion of the sea and the pull of tides than by changes in its level.

Today, the county of Suffolk owes much of its topography to these previous epochs. To the west, clay uplands and patches of deep chalk dominate the landscape. One of the last areas to be cleared of its ancient forests, this heavy land is now an important bread basket for the nation. The thick clay soils, brought to productive life by centuries of cultivation, manure and drainage, now generate tens of thousands of

tons of wheat each year. To the east, the highlands of the county are drained by a series of river valleys. Fed by both surface water and groundwater, these rivers slowly grow in stature. Most start as seasonal field drains or, more rarely, as springs. As the ditches and small inland tributaries converge, the flow of the rivers becomes more constant and they gain their names: the Stour, the Orwell and Gipping, the Deben, the Alde and Ore, the Blyth and the Waveney.

These rivers bring definition and meaning to the landscape through which they flow. They account for the lie of the land, the routes of ancient highways, the location of settlements and the character of the farm land. Moving from west to east, the soil grades from the heavy boulder clay on the high land through loam and meadowland on the sides of the river valleys to sand, alluvial soils and peat in the valley bottoms and along the coast. Here, the rivers broaden into wide, meandering estuaries, often snaking for miles through reclaimed farmland and heath before reaching the sea. Seen from above, the river valleys appear as long green fingers of pasture, flood meadows and woodland that extend far inland. Their flow, written lazily from source to the sea, penetrates the easternmost promontories of the Mid Suffolk uplands. They are the signature of the East Suffolk countryside.

In his book *Suffolk Scene*, Julian Tennyson devoted a whole chapter to the county's rivers. In passing over the eastern fringes of Suffolk, he described one small area in particular detail: the countryside that lies between the market towns of Framlingham and Saxmundham. This is the land of the Rivers Fromus, Ore and, tucked neatly between them, the Upper Alde.

> *"The villages along the valleys are small and sheltered, the country is quiet and deserted; it has a wildness that is rich and protected, almost soothing, quite different in its effect from that of the high plateau towards the Waveney. In some places you can take a standing jump over branches of the Alde; in summer I have seen them so dry that as streams they have ceased to exist at all, and in winter I have seen them rise and spread themselves across their valleys; but, no matter what state they are in, the country in between them has a distinct and gentle beauty of its own."*

The Upper Alde Valley, like the upper Fromus and Ore, is an intimate landscape. The river gathers itself together from ditches, springs and field drains above the villages of Badingham and Dennington. From there, it flows quietly through the parishes and villages of Bruisyard, Rendham, Sweffling, Great Glemham, Benhall, Stratford St Andrew and Farnham. Along its route, ancient pastures and flood meadows, often studded with old oak and ash trees, are fringed by marshy alder carr and grander plantations of oak. The grassland is grazed by beef cattle, sheep and a herd of dairy cows – now, sadly, a rarity in the area. Every now and again, the grass gives way to farmsteads and larger arable fields. These low lying sandy fields rotate through crops of barley, beans, peas, potatoes and beet – the wheat and oil seed rape tend to be concentrated on the heavier clay lands of the plateau. Running between the fields and farms along the river valley bottom, tarmac lanes connect the villages, intersecting with old footpaths, green lanes and the occasional farm track – sometimes these are left-overs of an ancient road that was made redundant by bridges built in the Middle Ages.

The villages stand separate, but close – none more than two miles from its neighbours. It is an ancient, long-settled landscape that has been continuously inhabited for tens of thousands of years. Farmsteads and scattered groups of cottages blur their boundaries. Names such as Red House Farm, White House Farm, Stone Farm, Hall Farm, Boundary Farm and Church Farm are repeated in many of the parishes. Within each village centre, short-towered flint and mortar churches, most dating from the 13th or 14th centuries, stand sentinel over their settlements. Trees now obscure many of the longer views in the Upper Alde Valley, but occasional glimpses suggest that the churches were all built on spots that afforded views up and down their parts of the valley. The churches of Stratford St Andrew and Farnham stand on either side of the threshold of the Upper Alde Valley; All Saints Church at Great Glemham has a long view to a hill above Farnham next to the A12 road, with shorter ones up and down its own smaller vale; Sweffling Church stands on the side of a steep (for Suffolk) hillock, while Rendham is a beacon for a broad swathe of land that spreads out from a bend in the river. And so it goes on, with the churches of Bruisyard, Badingham and Dennington tucked above the river in the upper reaches at the head of the valley. Beyond stretch the wild hinterlands of the Upper Alde.

If you look carefully, it becomes clear that amid the modern arrangements of roads, fields and woodland, almost all the villages are located at points in the valley that afford warmth, shelter, water, good soils and clear views, both upstream and downstream. Farnham, Stratford St Andrew, Sweffling, Rendham, Bruisyard, Badingham and Dennington all lie along the main stretch or run of the Upper Alde – if it can be called that. It is exceptionally quiet – a feature of almost all the county's rivers. At home, where my farm borders the Upper Alde, the loudest sound is from a small riffle set in the midst of a clump of water mint and rushes. If you stand quietly a few yards from the river you can hear its faint rippling trickle through the foliage. But if there is a breeze or you are further away, the sound is gone. I remember once pointing the river out to visitors from Wales, who had come to a farm event. We were a few hundred yards away, at the end of a long field that runs from the farmyards to the river. They paused to listen, but heard nothing, despite a favourable wind. "Where is the river?" they asked. I pointed it out again, "At the end of the field, a few hundred yards." "But you can't hear it," they replied. Compared to the cascades of Wales, Cumbria and Scotland, Suffolk's rivers are exceptionally discreet. Here, apart from the sounds of A12 traffic, farm machinery, cows blooring, dogs barking and bells, it is still a quiet country, largely dark at night.

The village of Great Glemham stands slightly set back from the Alde in a smaller valley or vale drained by its own tiny tributary. Known variously as the gull, groop, beck or stream, it is not grand enough to have a formal name. Although it is always full with slow-flowing groundwater near the main river, the upper reaches are effectively a very large field drain. They receive water from several square miles of uplands, but most run-off is absorbed by intervening patches of loamy meadow land and sand. It is generally only in winter, when the land becomes full and saturated,

that the flow fills the gull. As in other parts of the valley, resurgent woodland now obscures the local topography for much of the year. But in winter the position and orientation of Great Glemham in its local landscape become more apparent.

The village church, All Saints, stands at the top of the Street, a short double row of red brick cottages. Some of these have hidden within them foundations and frames from the 16th and 17th centuries. Now all residential properties, they once included a forge, a butcher, a cobbler's workshop and a village stores. To the south west, the Street gives way to farmland and open countryside, punctuated by a series of outlying farmsteads - Red House Farm, Church Farm, Trust Farm, Potash, Paul's

Grove and Stone Farm. To the north, the Street drops down a slight hill and passes the village pub (The Crown Inn). It then bends sharply left, becoming the Low Road. This runs past the Village Hall, a number of newer houses, the former School (built by the Duke of Hamilton and still bearing his crest) and the Street Farm (previously the home of Hugh Barrett and mentioned in the last chapter of his book *A Good Living*). The road then runs for a mile or so beside the gull (overlooked by Red House Farm, Church Farm, Trust Farm, Potash, Paul's Grove and Stone Farm) before reaching Pound Farm and a new 200-acre wood planted by

the Woodland Trust. From there it heads uphill towards the A1120, Cransford and Framlingham.

Opposite the pub at a T-junction, a side road heads north up a long hill *, becoming Chapel Lane. On the left side of the lane is the site of the former village garage, once owned by Mr Cyril Quantrill (who organised trips in an old Austin to Framlingham on market days). This is followed by the former Methodist chapel (also built by the Duke of Hamilton), from which the road gets its name, and a cluster of new homes. On the right side of the road is the old parsonage, another larger group of newer houses and a converted barn. Beyond this the road once again passes through open countryside, wending its way towards Hall Farm between arable fields called Barnfield, Horse Hill, Jordans, Rook Street, Longfield and Longfield Cottages. These are all enclosures of heavy clay land, under-drained, mole-drained and subsoiled. Beneath the hedges that extend along their lower margins, deep field ditches carry rainwater down past the new homes and the old parsonage to the gull – in

* I write this with apologies to readers for whom a hill needs to have both a steep incline and, perhaps more importantly, a summit. Inclines, and therefore hills, certainly exist in Suffolk. They are a common feature in the local landscape – a fact that can be easily checked by watching which way water runs along a road when it is raining. But summits are more elusive. They exist, but it is difficult to pin them down to any area smaller than a few acres of heavy upland clay.

winter they become small torrents, far noisier than the distant River Alde into which they eventually empty.

Back at the bottom of the village hill, opposite the pub and just beside the T-junction, there is another opening – a wide sandy gateway between two square columns set within a long red brick wall. To the left, the wall extends down the hill towards the gull and the parsonage, stopping after a hundred yards or so. It used to carry on up to the stream, joining the side of the brick bridge, but a great flood in the 1930s knocked it down. Before the final section of the wall collapsed, the floodwaters had reached the first floor of a row of cottages next to the old garage. At the request of local residents it was never rebuilt. On the other side of the gateway, the red brick wall continues up towards the main Street for a hundred yards before turning left and running along a lane called the New Road. At the end of this straight stretch of about 300 yards, two small lanes approach from the north and south, converging to form a cross-roads. A metal signpost stands to one side of the junction beneath a grove of wild cherries. Its arms point to Farnham, Stratford St Andrew, Sweffling, Rendham, Little Glemham, Great Glemham and Framlingham. Here the wall makes another left turn and runs a further two hundred yards, until it meets a second road bridge over the gull, terminating in another square-built column.

A series of initials are engraved on bricks just before the bridge: AB and RSW. The author of the first inscription is A. Barham, and a date marks the year 1871, in which the Duke of Hamilton bought the land that the long wall conceals. RSW stands for Ronald Sidney Watling, who rebuilt numerous sections of the wall after the Great Storm of 1987. His initials can be found in many farm buildings in Great Glemham and his workmanship will have kept many of them standing for years to come. Beyond the bridge stands a two-storey flint gatehouse called The Lodge. Further back on the New Road a diamond pattern of darker bricks marks the original mid-point of the wall, before the flood bit off a section by the first bridge in the village. A larger patch of cleaner red bricks near the diamond marks the spot at which a B17 Flying Fortress crashed in 1943.

The sandy gateway opposite the pub opens into a short private drive of raw flint and sand. This is the entrance to a group of buildings known collectively as the Timber Yard. Below the drive, behind oak trees and young elms, lie an old saw pit, workshop, dovecote and stable block – the latter now converted to a row of cottages with striking 18th century pediment and brickwork. Beyond these is an expanse of flat parkland, through which the gull has been canalised. Just as the North Sea endlessly alters the shoreline of Suffolk along its soft eroding coast, the gull rearranges itself during its winter surges: the remains of wooden bracing and sandstone flags that line the gull appear and disappear in the shifting sands. A pair of goalposts that stood on the park above the stream in the 1970s have gone, but two ancient stag-headed chestnut trees survive, the rotted heartwood of one pock-marked with holes left by musket balls. Nearby a lime tree, a century or two younger than the sweet chestnuts, and knocked down in the 1987 storm, has carried on growing regardless, with a trunk that mimics the route of the long red brick wall, turning a full ninety degrees along its length. The force of the hurricane heaved its trunk and rootplate out of the ground, leaving the latter upended in a large crumbling lump of dark podzolic subsoil.

In good years the grassland around the buildings and old trees at the Timber Yard – known as the Low Park – produces abundant quantities of hay or silage. But in drought years, the sward is liable to burn up and wither on the light free-draining loam that lies beneath it. In the driest years of all, faint patterns appear on a patch of elevated ground east of the stable block cottages. They trace lumps and lines of dryness in the earth, suggesting that something lies buried beneath the surface: perhaps the remains of a larger building that seems so conspicuous by its absence from the cluster of old stables, saw pit, workshop, stream and ancient chestnut trees. These scorch marks are thought to mark the footprint of Great Glemham Hall, once owned by the North family of Little Glemham Hall (Earls of Guildford). All that survives is a faint sketch of the building in the Fitch Collection – a compact three and a half storey Tudor mansion arranged in a classic E-shape form, with mullion

windows and tall brick chimney stacks.

Between 1796 and 1801 Dudley North, the owner of Little Glemham Hall, let the house to Suffolk's gritty poet George Crabbe and his family. George Crabbe junior described the setting in his biography *The Poetical Works of the Rev George Crabbe with his Letters and Journals, and his Life, by his Son* (1834):

> *"A small well-wooded park occupied the whole mouth of the glen, whence, doubtless, the name of the village was derived. In the lowest ground stood the commodious mansion; the approach wound down through a plantation on the eminence in front. The opposite hill rose at the back of it, rich and varied with trees and shrubs scattered irregularly; under this southern hill ran a brook, and on the banks above it were spots of great natural beauty, enthroned by whitethorn and oak … In fact, the whole parish and neighbourhood resemble a combination of groves, interspersed with fields cultivated like gardens, and intersected with those green lanes which tempt the walker in all weathers."*

The picture he creates is vivid and today many key components of the landscape survive. The wooded eminence in front still exists, although it is now occupied largely by a spinney of young sycamore and beech trees and a growing colony of rooks. The opposite hill is still *"enthroned by whitethorn and oak*" – including a hawthorn stump of immense antiquity. A good number of the fields that surround the village centre also survive in an arrangement that would be recognisable from the late 18th century: Mill Mount, Kiln Piece, Church Field, Dry Hill, Cemetery, Second Church, Dairy Maid, Bachelors, Church Farm Meadow, Goose Hill, Ruffords and School Field – a roll call of village history. But there are also huge differences: the old meandering highway has gone, replaced by the New Road; the gull has been straightened and now flows only in winter; and, most obvious of all, the "*commodious mansion*" that

lay in the middle of this setting, Great Glemham Hall, has disappeared, demolished in 1806.

The building that replaced the Hall was a much larger and grander dwelling with the more modest name of Glemham House. The House and, in particular, its garden are the subject of this book. Looking up from the site of Crabbe's mansion in a northerly direction, the land rises to a small eastern promontory of the uplands of mid-Suffolk. The landscape features that surround the Timber Yard provide clues to the history and design of the new house. The New Road derives its name from a long-forgotten adjustment that straightened the public highway from an older meandering route. This paved the way for the subsequent enclosure of 120 acres of pasture, fields and woodland as a new park. The remains of timbers and flagstones in the gull probably date from the same period. They too provide proof of a deliberate re-working of the landscape on a large scale. The positions of the younger trees on the flat pasture around the former site of Great Glemham Hall also only make sense in a broader landscape setting that contains views that reach far beyond the boundaries of the Timber Yard.

Move three hundred yards east and downstream, and all these alterations to the landscape begin to make sense: the gull flows out into the bed of a large two-acre lake with oak trees, an old tea house and the remains of a boat house at the far end; beyond the lake, to the north and north east, the flat pasture of the Timber Yard opens into a wide expanse of sloping land dotted with large-crowned oak, sycamore and conker trees; and at the top of the hill stands the new building itself, Glemham House. With the landscape re-balanced to frame this new property, the land around the Timber Yard became the Low Park to the south west of Glemham House, with Front Park, Lodge Hill, Linen Ground, Back Park and North Hill surrounding it to the south, east, north and west – enclosed to the south by the long red brick wall with the diamond near its middle and RSW at one end.

Built between 1813 and 1823, the new house was commissioned by Samuel Kilderbee Esq, a town clerk and businessman from Ipswich. After his death in 1814, the house and parkland became the property of his son, the Rev. Dr Samuel Kilderbee. Following his father's plans, the younger Kilderbee created the greatly expanded parkland setting with classic features of the late Regency period: lake and parkland; shrubberies; ice house; dovecote; entrance lodge; servants' accommodation and service wing; stables; coach house and vegetable garden. The older buildings at the Timber Yard were absorbed into this larger landscape setting through the careful planting of new groves of trees and parkland oaks, the former stable block becoming a bailiff's house and a polygonal dovecote a scenic feature within the new landscape.

The house has changed hands several times. It was bought by the Duke of Hamilton in 1871 for his honeymoon. Forty-two years later it was bought by my great-grandparents the 3rd Earl and Countess of Cranbrook, Gathorne and Dorothy Gathorne-Hardy. It has remained our main family home ever since, filled with three subsequent generations of Cranbrooks and Gathorne-Hardys. Despite these successive changes in ownership nearly all the principal elements of its late Regency design have survived intact, with subsequent innovations or improvements appearing as additions rather than wholesale alterations. The principal rooms of the house face south and overlook the front park and lake. On its northern side, there is a long low wing of service quarters, next to a compact stable courtyard. Originally, these buildings contained ground floor kitchens, a laundry, still room, coach house and stables. Above these, the first floor accommodation was subdivided into rooms for staff. There was also a garden cottage and a hayloft. The house was built as a small village unto itself, designed to be self-sufficient in food and water, with all activity geared to support the family of the owners and their servants. But times change. The staff

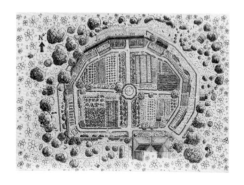

accommodation and some of the former service wing have been converted to apartments, though the laundry (with two large coppers and slatted wooden window) and stables remain unmodernised. The residents are now tenant householders and neighbours rather than employees of the house. Other rooms have also changed function. A former stable for coaching horses was converted by my great-grandfather to a diesel-powered engine room. The generator provided low-voltage electricity for the house – and left a room stained with thick black soot. (The ceiling was covered with scratched graffiti left by soldiers billeted to the house in the 1940s and by myself, siblings and friends in the 1970s.)

To the north of the stable yard, a large walled kitchen garden covers almost two acres. Viewed from above, it has the appearance of a squashed nine-sided polygon, the southern sections of its walls compressed and flattened. Its northern and western flanks are fringed by a deep belt of shrubberies – a mixture of mature oak, beech, lime, walnut and chestnut trees under-planted with laurels, yew, holly and various evergreen shrubs. In winter these are carpeted with drifts of snowdrops, aconites and, a month or two later, daffodils and patches of bluebells. To the west, a path from the shrubberies connects to the wooded Dell – a deep-set path that cuts through a bank of heavy clay and chalky marl to lead visitors downhill towards the Timber Yard and Great Glemham pub. To the south, the shrubberies give way to apple orchards and an area of ornamental trees and shrubs. These in turn frame a series of lawns that surround the family part of the main house.

With up to 30 staff, family members and visitors living on site at any one time in the 19th century, the house was built to be semi-independent, operating much like a large ship. It had highly structured chains of command and a constant need for supplies of

food, water, fuel and power. In the early 19th century, fuel would have been mainly coal. There are more than 40 open fires, stoves, boilers and associated chimney pots in the house and outbuildings, all of which would have provided heat and hot water in the early to mid 19th century. Later, a small gas works was built in a pit in the park. This supplied coal gas for

domestic lighting in the second half of the 19th century – the pit survives as the Gas Pit. (As a child I remember finding odd bits of glass valves and metal, but the rest of the works had gone.) It was replaced by the diesel-powered generator that once stood in the engine room. Again, the machinery has been removed, but a large concrete pedestal and enormous fat transmission cables survived. It wasn't until 1947 that mains electricity reached the house.

Water was supplied by a complex system of wells, pumps and large water tanks (for holding rainwater). Sales particulars for the house in 1829 describe a good supply of "soft water". This was probably stored rainwater (modern mains water is notoriously hard in East Suffolk). The power for the water pumps – and for almost all other domestic activities that concerned washing, cooking and movement of foods or fuel around the buildings – would originally have been provided by the hard graft of employees, ranging in age from early teens to late seventies. As new fuels and motors arrived, there would have been a slow but steady transition to mechanical power provided by combustion engines and, later, electricity.

In terms of fuel, power and labour, the internal functioning of the main house can be seen as following a familiar path blazed by the broader

industrial revolution of the mid 19th and early 20th centuries, with progressive shifts in fuels and energy sources and increasing mechanization of domestic processes. But self-sufficiency was still of paramount importance – to the extent that the house even developed its own micro-power stations for gas and electricity. The air must have been quite noxious on still winter days – it is easy to forget just how polluting coal fires were. This may have been an additional reason for Samuel Kilderbee to locate his new house in its elevated position, benefiting from beautiful views and the cleansing effect of strong south-westerly winds. Certainly this scale of smoke in a poorly ventilated location would have been a far cry from the Regency fashion for

"... what was beautiful, productive and well-loved, like Donwel Abbey in Emma or Colonel Brandon's 'nice old fashioned place' in Sense and Sensibility that Mrs Jennings so admires: the great garden walls that are covered with the very best fruit trees in the country; and such a mulberry tree in one corner! Then there is the dovecote, some delightful stewponds and a very pretty canal; and everything, in short, that one could wish for."

(From Mavis Batey's *Regency Gardens*)

Looking at this description, it is clear that in creating Glemham House in its new position on a small rise overlooking the Upper Alde Valley and the vale of Great Glemham, Kilderbee managed to pull it all together: a south-facing country house in an elevated position with parkland, rolling approach, timber yard, dovecote, stables, canalised stream, lake, shrubberies, stables, lawns and walled kitchen garden. Today, at the start of the 21st century – almost 200 years after Glemham House was

completed and first launched into existence – it is the *"great garden walls"* that define it. Setting aside the plumes of coal smoke that must have once adorned its many chimneys, the walled garden remains the productive heart of the house and has been in continuous use since 1823.

At first glance, the position of the kitchen garden in the local landscape defies common gardening sense: a two-acre enclosure on heavy boulder clay on an exposed north-east promontory of the Suffolk uplands is almost the worst conceivable location for a large domestic vegetable garden. But this anomalous situation is what makes it so fascinating. Our Mesolithic ancestors, the Celtic Trinovantes and Iceni, the Romans and possibly their Anglo-Saxon successors all knew the difficulty of raising food crops from clay land – they restricted most of their cultivation to the softer soils of the hill sides and valley edges, avoiding the heavy clay outwash of the plateau.

Yet, there it is, the kitchen garden, laid out in its irregular beauty on this most unlikely of sites: four slightly asymmetric quarters of vegetable patches bisected by a broad central promenade fringed by wide herbaceous borders; a central basin or dipping pond; three ancient greenhouses containing peach, nectarine, apricot, lemon and vines; a fourth modern aluminium greenhouse, overflowing with pelargoniums and a fiercely vigorous Malaysian lime tree; a fruit cage sheltering raspberries, gooseberries, currants and espaliered apples and pears; a higgledy-piggledy array of veteran fruit trees (a cankerous Lord Derby, a spindly Lord Suffield and, among others, a resplendent Annie Elizabeth – invigorated after being upended in 1987); a wooden well-house; a

potting shed; an apple store; a barrow and ladder shed (formerly a mushroom shed); the gardener's bothy and the remains of old boiler rooms.

Each and every year since it was first enclosed in the 1820s, this patch of ground has produced sufficient food to sustain 30 or 40 people. During parts of the 19th and early 20th centuries, it would certainly have been doing this for the family and staff. In the 1940s, production may have dropped, for the house was requisitioned by the army and my grandparents moved to White House Farm, about half a mile away. They still maintained the garden, but there were fewer employees to work on it and to "Dig for Victory". Any shortfall would have been more than compensated by a new market garden on the edge of the original parkland (on a field known variously as the Bird Ground or Budding Ground) managed with help from the Women's Land Army. This raises a question: if the underlying soil is so poor, how has the garden managed to remain productive for almost two hundred years? The answer seems to lie in its design. On closer viewing, it becomes clear that almost every aspect and detail of the kitchen garden is organised around one guiding principle: to concentrate the goodness of soil, sunshine, water and manure for the growth of fruit and vegetables.

The walls, over twelve feet tall and up to four bricks thick, are high enough to trap a micro-climate of air inside the garden, even allowing for the eddying effect of a stiff breeze overhead. They form a nine-sided polygon, but this shape is squashed on its north-south axis to form an irregular slightly hemi-circular enclosure, with a straight section of wall along the south-west edge. This ensures that the maximum length of internal wall has a southerly aspect. The mature oak, beech and lime trees in the shrubberies, criss-crossed with quiet scenic walks beneath, extend in a long arc around the back of the kitchen garden to create a tall amphitheatre of trees behind the north-west, north and north-east margins of the walled garden. This acts as a second windbreak, further enhancing the local micro-climate; but more importantly, it buffers the garden against the north-easterly winds in winter, which can be bitingly cold. Beneath the surface, the entire two acres within the garden seem to have been excavated to a depth of three or four feet and under-drained. A layer of clinker was then laid down (in some areas – we are not

sure how extensive this is) and a deep layer of imported top soil was probably deposited on top and spread over the surface. The circular dipping pond in the middle of the garden was (until 1987) fed by gravity from a large deep oval pond situated 150 yards away at the back of the shrubberies – itself filled by land drains extending over four acres of heavy clay parkland. In addition to this, all rainwater falling

on to the greenhouses was (and is still) collected via gutters and down pipes in a series of deep brick-lined water troughs (populated by duckweed, frogs and water boatmen). Inside the greenhouses, additional warmth was provided in winter months by a complex network of huge cast iron pipes. These conveyed hot water and steam from subterranean boiler rooms, one set underground within the walls of the garden and one outside. Tools were stored in a potting shed and a mushroom shed; produce was stored in an apple and root store – or taken inside to be bedded down in slate-lined storage bins filled with sand.

These design elements provide a relatively stable enclosure for gardening – an oasis almost. But warmth, suntraps, adequate supplies of water, a deep tilth and good storage facilities would not have been sufficient by themselves to ensure the kitchen garden's productivity. Two additional resources would have been essential: muck and knowledge. From talking to my parents and reading gardeners' diaries, I know that every year for the past 40 years over six tons of farmyard manure has gone into the soil in the garden in a single-depth digging. Cumulatively, that amounts to over 240 tons of muck. If this rate of application is extended back to 1823, it is possible that over 1,100 tons of manure or compost have been dug into the two acres of top soil that fill the walled garden, sometimes double-dug to a depth of two spade blades. Before the arrival of water closets and lavatories in the house and gardener's bothy, the annual input of manure was probably complemented by large amounts of night soil and leaf mould, the latter collected in abundance from the shrubberies.

If putting good quantities of well-composted organic waste into the soil provides a sound foundation for production, it is knowledge or folklore that makes the ground productive. Knowing what to plant when and how to nurture it thereafter is as important as a good top-dressing:

it enables the investment in time, sweat and effort to bear fruit. But this knowledge is hard to come by and easily lost. At Great Glemham, my mother has since 1971 kept notes of her seed orders and the success of different varieties (a list of suppliers is in Appendix II). These records are complemented by the diaries and recorded recollections of gardeners who have worked at Glemham House over the years: Tom Eley, Julie Paternoster, George Smith, Charles Chandler, David Coles, Alan Sharpe, Stewart Cousins, Keith Saunders, Robert Camp and Christopher Ellis.

All brought extensive personal knowledge to the garden, often sharing it with my parents, family and visitors.

It was into this setting – a two-acre late Regency walled kitchen garden populated by my parents, family members, staff, relatives, visitors, friends and many plants with curious histories - that the artist Tessa Newcomb came to paint in 2006.

* * *

"They sat and smoked in silence for a while. All their interest in the fields that flew past them had faded: they were both thinking of Crakenhill. Suddenly Bob looked up. 'I say,' he said impulsively, 'let's go back, Hiram.' Hiram nodded. 'P'raps it'd be better,' he replied."

THIS EXCERPT IS from *Joseph and His Brethren* by H W Freeman. The book is set in the parish of Badingham, a few miles upstream of Great Glemham in the Upper Alde Valley. It describes two brothers, Bob and Hiram, on their way to Canada. They are running away to a new life. No one at home at Crakenhill Farm knows. They have bought tickets at Ipswich train station, where they have learned that travelling to Canada means changing at Peterborough in order to go on to Liverpool. After what must be barely ten or twenty minutes, they are farther from home than they have ever been in their lives. As they look at the new fields passing by, their minds and conversation both turn to their own farm: its crops, the hay and their horses. What will happen to them?

Who will look after them? It is all too much. They jump out at the next station and head for home, walking through the night.

This pull of the land is something that I have felt many times in my own life. At times it is a pull away, an attraction to new places – to Borneo, Ireland and the windswept hills of Scotland (where hills have the luxury of having both inclines and summits). At other times it is a

yearning for familiar places seen afresh: the Howgill Fells around Sedbergh in Cumbria; the wooded valleys of mid Wales; or the rural landscape of West Malaysia. But it can also express itself as a sense of peace or being at ease in a landscape that feels alive and active, doing its own thing: a forested catchment area in the Highlands of Borneo; a patch of rough, tussocky grassland at home on my farm in Suffolk; or a boggy fell in the north-west of England.

I came into the world in 1968 in a small place called Gombak in the jungle just north of Kuala Lumpur. My father had left England in 1956 to work as Technical Assistant at the Sarawak Museum with Tom Harrisson. He came back 15 year later with my mother, myself, aged two years old, and a parrot called Wipim. When my parents returned to England in 1970, my grandparents, Jock and Fidelity Cranbrook (the Fourth Earl and Countess of Cranbrook) had already moved to a much smaller house at Red House Farm on the edge of the village. My sister Flora and brother Argus were born soon after this to

complete the family, together with a long line of pet dogs, guinea pigs, tailless gerbils, horses, ponies, stick insects, tree frogs and several hundred Madeiran wolf spiders – Wipim retired to London Zoo, as did the spiders.

There is an external freedom that comes from physical movement and travel. But there is also a deeper or quieter freedom that can grow within one's life: an inner freedom to treat the familiar as new, the old as fresh. This can take more time and the path can be unclear. But of the two modes of travelling, it is perhaps the more liberating one, for it allows the unexpected to come into one's life, germinate, take root and flourish. I had the happy accident of being born in Malaysia – a country or homeland which deep friendships and family connections have many times taken me back to (mainly to Sarawak, and to Kuching and Bario in the Kelabit Highlands in particular). Academically, I started my travels at Framlingham Primary School, before continuing studies at Woodbridge School and the University of Oxford. After abandoning postgraduate academia, I started working as a painter. My interest was the land and how it worked and I painted it with materials from the landscape. It seemed the most natural way to work: to pick up soil in one hand, plants in the

other, and to use them as pigments and tools. Between 1995 and 1998, I also attended Maggi Hambling's life drawing classes at Morley College in London, learning the vital importance of observation and, perhaps more essential still, to be true to one's gifts and skills. It was at this time that I began to exhibit at galleries in London and East Anglia (Reeds Wharf Gallery, the Barbican, Snape Maltings Concert Hall Gallery, Aldeburgh Cinema Gallery, the Peter Pears Gallery in Aldeburgh and the Redfern Gallery in London).

Returning to Suffolk in 2002, I began to explore what was happening locally. I saw Tessa's work (both in East Anglia and at the Crane Kalman Gallery in London). Her paintings were full of the landscape and also the quirks of Suffolk – pink cottages punctuating country views, allotments, black-tarred fishermen's huts on beaches and birds singing from bare branches in spring time. I was renovating a cottage at the time and asked if she would paint murals in it depicting Great Glemham. She accepted the commission and spent several weeks painting scenes from the village Street and surrounding countryside. The project generated local interest and we decided to open the house for a few weeks when the commission was completed. This became the first Easter Retreat Exhibition. The following year, we repeated it in my farmhouse. The third year it grew again and I moved the exhibition into

the farm's lambing sheds, where it has remained, expanding year by year.

At the same time, I was putting on solo shows of my own work, mainly drawings of sea birds, livestock and people working in the landscape. In 2003 and 2004 I held two exhibitions of drawings from Suffolk. The first was downstairs in the Redfern Gallery on Cork Street in London. The second was at Snape Maltings Concert Hall Gallery overlooking the Alde estuary – one of the first places I had visited with books and boards to paint with muds and plants. Given that almost all the work for both exhibitions came from the Alde Valley, I thought it would be appropriate to open them with a selection of dishes prepared from fresh seasonal farmed and wild foods from the Alde Valley, prepared by friend and cook Claire Bruce-Clayton (co-owner of the award-winning Lawsons Delicatessen in Aldeburgh).

At the opening of the Snape exhibition another friend, Paul Thomas, approached me. He had recently opened a café at Marlesford on the A12 trunk road which specialised in locally sourced foods, with a famous Suffolk Breakfast. He said he liked the drawings but "loved the grub". This comment left me intrigued. It also raised the question: could food events be managed and held in the same way as art events, combining information and experience? Six months later, I launched

Below: Basket making in Pa Umor, Pesta Nukenen Bario, Sarawak, 2010

The Alde Valley Food Adventures at Paul's farm café with a menu of 30 dishes made by two chefs using ingredients almost entirely sourced from within 10 miles of the café. This became the start of a rolling programme of Food Adventures that roved up and down the Alde Valley, to London and then to Malaysia. A few months later, I found myself sitting beside the airstrip in Bario in the Heart of Borneo, where I met John Tarawe, a friend and manager of the Kelabit Highland community's solar hybrid powered E-Bario Telecentre. After telling me that artists were notoriously unreliable characters, I showed John some menu sheets from the Alde Valley Food Adventures, including the launch event at the farm café. John looked at them and said that he thought the model – which was designed to help protect and celebrate local food and landscape identity – could be applied in Bario.

Today, the Easter Retreat Exhibition has grown into The Alde Valley Spring Festival, a four-week celebration of food, farming, landscape and the arts in the Alde Valley and beyond. It takes place at my farm, just down hill from Glemham House. The Food Adventures continue to develop as a programme of intermittent events, combined with research into foods, identity and socio-economic policy. In Malaysia, Pesta Nukenen Bario (The Bario and Kelabit Highlands Food and Cultural Festival) has taken root. After two pioneering years of stewardship under the management of the E-Bario Telecentre staff, the festival was given to the Kelabit Highland's Kaum Ibu women's group. Under their care it has grown year-on-year and achieved financial independence in 2010. My role has shifted and I now work as the patron on a voluntary basis, helping with inward funding and international partnerships – promoting the extraordinary food, forest and cultural heritage of the Kelabit Highlands. One of the last intact traditionally farmed and forested

Highland catchment areas in Sarawak, it is tragically at risk from logging.

These experiences, in conjunction with an ongoing programme of small Knowledge Fairs launched by the community in the Highlands and University Malaysia Sarawak (UNIMAS), led me to conclude that the practice of gardening and the knowledge that goes with it are of fundamental importance to the well-being of individuals and communities. Smaller projects held during the Alde Valley Spring Festivals of 2010 and 2011 both revealed an additional need in East Suffolk: to facilitate the release of land for gardening, allotments and community-supported agriculture. This seems to be a global trend: people need land.

It was during this time that Tessa first suggested painting in the kitchen garden at Glemham House, partly as an extension to work she was already doing about allotments in local towns and villages. Given the nature of the kitchen garden – with its tall polygonal walls and four entrances it often feels like a theatre or stage – it seemed worthwhile to set this up as an informal residency with a dedicated exhibition at the end of it. But as the seasons rolled by and the number of paintings, drawings and sketches increased, we began to think that a selling exhibition at the end of the residency period would be too sudden an end to the project: additional stories, thoughts and observations would be lost as soon as the paintings were sold and dispersed. This led to the idea of producing a book about the residency project, with Tessa's work telling the story of the garden through the seasons. We put together a proposal for Full Circle Editions in 2009, which they accepted.

This book is the result. In writing it, I hope I will be able to convey some of the atmosphere, energy and activity that run through the garden at different times of year, complementing Tessa's beautiful paintings and sketches. I have divided it into 12 chapters, one for each calendar month of the year. These are illustrated by Tessa's drawings and paintings, made through the seasons during 2008, 2009 and 2010. I have started each chapter with some of Tessa's own words and a checklist of Garden Notes. These have been collated from the working diaries of Alan Sharpe, Stewart Cousins, Keith Saunders and Chris Ellis, who have all helped manage the gardens at Glemham House during the past 10 years. Their notes, edited by my parents, provide glimpses into the daily and seasonal workings of the garden.

The narrative that follows the Garden Notes takes the form of my own recollections and observations. Sometimes these wander away from the narrow borders of the garden to explore themes that relate to its location, history and design – and to the many extraordinary threads of oral history that connect the garden to the local landscape and to local social history. But I have sought always to return to the stage within the tall walls and to the vegetable beds, sheds and greenhouses. At the end of each chapter I have included a selection of recipes for produce, either fresh or stored, that comes into the house in that particular month. These have been contributed by family, friends and chefs with whom it has been both an honour and the greatest delight to share cooking time, recipes and meals over the past few years. Some are recipes that have been used for Food Adventures or Alde Valley Spring Festival events; others are dishes that I have seen or tried at friends' homes, or on menus at pubs, cafés or restaurants. My hope is that these will bridge the gap between the garden and the home, or the kitchen.

At the end of the book you will find a set of appendices that provide

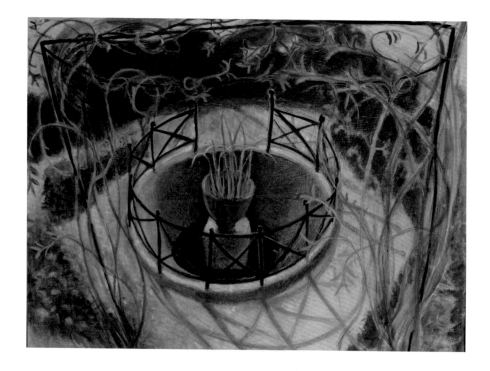

more information about the history of gardeners at Glemham House, growing food for the house, seed suppliers, some recipes for spring weeds and a sample of Suffolk dialect. There is also a short bibliography, in case you want to explore some of the references that underpinned the writing. But the written content is only part of the story; it is the accompaniment to Tessa's beautiful work. The watercolours, sketches and oil paintings that illustrate the book represent the culmination of three years spent watching, observing, drawing and painting in the kitchen garden at Great Glemham. It is a remarkable record of the changing seasons and the carefully planned cycle of activities that make up daily life in the garden. It was a great pleasure to see them come into being, and a greater pleasure to be able to share her work in this way, in printed form.

Jason Gathorne-Hardy

IT WAS A GOOD TIME for me – drawing in the garden. I would drive 10 miles there, enter the theatre, which is how I saw the garden, talk to the gardener, draw – because I knew the setting it was easy to focus on the changes – then go home carrying the images in my mind as well as in my bag as drawings. I would stop outside the gates to write down sentences which are apt to float away, then home to fix the memories in paint.

I visited every few weeks. The gardener would update me on what had happened. I felt very grand, as if everything had been done for me. Within those walls everything was the same but also utterly different. Sometimes it was "all earth", and it seemed impossible. Sometimes it was beautiful. I would float down the herbaceous borders high with Michaelmas daisies and cabbage whites.

Drawing fixes me in one place. Things happen. A green shield beetle crawls across the green sundial. The midday sun moves the shadow round the garlic patch. A cloud moves across the sky.

I've always thought of painting as "time not lost". You are saving it from slipping away. Since my time in the walled garden I have felt that all time I spend in gardens I'm noticing, documenting, storing information for a reason.

It was a time of intense concentration, one that changed me.

Tessa Newcomb

January

The sky is clear
It's going to drop to minus three & snow 'til Thursday
Must not wilt.
Inside the apple store apples decay and stay gold in the gloom.
Sunday morning, the bells are ringing.

Tessa Newcomb

This page: Rose hips

January

Garden Notes

Clear herbaceous borders. Set bonfires to burn waste wood in the Dell and Shrubberies. Prune and tie back roses. Clean chilli house. Chop firewood and re-fill wood stores. Move chrysanthemums from house, cut back and place in chilli house. Continue digging vegetable beds. Put wood ash and chicken muck on asparagus, artichokes and raspberries. Set mouse traps in apple store. Set up netting over broccoli, kale and winter greens to keep off pigeons. Sort apple store – throw out rotten apples to birds and chickens. Check cabbages in the store. Water chickens and clear out the run; stock with fresh sand and straw. Order seeds from catalogues.

I REMEMBER an afternoon spent walking along the northern shore of the River Stour at Stutton on the Suffolk-Essex border. The tide had turned and the river, a broad estuary, was creeping back inland from the sea. Hundreds of acres of mudflats that had lain bare for half a day bubbled quietly as briny water slipped into half-buried burrows made by lugworms and cockles, forcing out little pockets of trapped air. Wherever the level of the mud dropped just a fraction, it formed tiny bays. The roving front of the tide would rush into these small depressions and then pause, its advance arrested until each minute lagoon was full. Then it would race on, lifting moulted feathers and seaweed from the mud. The progress of the tide, which looked so gradual, smooth and even from afar, was in fact a hiccupping run of stops and starts when viewed close up from the water's edge.

January often feels like this – a returning tide. The true depths of winter, in terms of darkness and daylight, have already passed. Each day after the winter solstice is a little bit longer and, as a rule, brighter than the one before. High up in the sky the daily ration of sunlight is growing step by step in a smooth, orderly progression. But on the ground, close to the soil in the garden, it can be a very different matter. Sometimes everything just stops. Whole days hang in the air like damp rags, wet to the face. The high walls of the garden become the rim of a pool filled with soft mist, stirred gently by slow internal currents. Time unwinds. The light of early morning seems no different from that at dusk. Beyond the walls, trees in the apple orchards and shrubberies stand as hazy silhouettes, drifting in and out of view. On the rich soil of the vegetable beds, softened by frosts, surviving red cabbages stand like scarred soldiers on a battlefield, their leaves withered and ruptured from frost and rain. Nearby on the fruit cage, a mesh of chicken wire and gossamer threads of spiders' webs both gather microscopic lenses of dew. Such is the stillness and thickness of moisture in the air that even the most familiar sounds seem overly loud: the hourly chime of the stable yard clock (now harnessed to an electronic bell); the startled alarm calls of blackbirds; cockerels crowing to each other across the shrubberies; or small dogs barking at the sound of a car on the distant drive.

And then, just as it seems that the whole world is on hold, the weather wakes up and moves on. Mists that are not blown away crystallise as hoar frosts or condense and fall as rain, sleet and snow. Underground, the dark earth of the garden remains warm and full of life, but above ground the air temperature can buck about wildly. Atlantic winds from the south west bring mild weather. But when they swing round and blow in from the north east, the temperature plummets. With no mountains to speak of between Suffolk and Siberia, the mercury can fall to minus ten degrees Celsius or even lower in its algae-covered gauge. At these temperatures, pea gravel on the paths consolidates into frozen lumps of pebbles and snow – like gritty nougat or brown bread ice cream. Suffolk Woolpit bricks that line the herbaceous borders grow rounded corners of ice. And the vegetable beds gain a frozen crust as hard as stone. In such weather December's

jobs – principally digging and pruning – are abandoned and activity in
the garden retreats to places of relative warmth: the potting shed and
the apple store.

The latter stands as an oddity. Almost every other aspect of the
walled garden's design has been carefully laid out to trap water and
light, and to gather warmth. In doing so, it nurtures the growth of
plants that live within it. The apple store is designed to do the opposite.
Arranged as a long low room on the north side of a north wall, it is a
shadowy dormitory for fruit and vegetables; a cool, dark store room.
Heavy wooden shutters cover slatted windows with no glass. When
these are down, only the faintest slivers of natural light penetrate the
gloom. There is no heating – only the warmth of the ground, a layer of

brick pammets laid on sand. Until recently, there was no electricity. To see anything at all, the shutters had to be carefully lifted and latched to a series of hand-forged iron hooks that hang beak-like from the ceiling. I remember the struggle of doing this as a child, standing on a bucket or up-ended wooden fruit box to lift the shutter with one arm, while reaching for the hook with the other. The price of a bucket of apples for the house or rotten fruit for blackbirds was sometimes a banged head.

Everything about the apple store is designed to decelerate and quieten the metabolism of plants. It is a store not for seedlings, but for fruits, roots, bulbs and the plump heads of cabbages and sprouts. Onions, shallots and heads of garlic are arranged in wooden and grey plastic trays on a long shelf just inside the shuttered windows. Opposite these (the storeroom is long and thin, almost barge-like in its dimensions) lines of apples and late pears are set out on two tiers of open-slatted wooden shelves. They are arranged in rows about an inch apart. The separation is vital to avoid the spread of rot. When you look along the full length of the apple store, the fruit have the appearance of old-fashioned army regiments, each variety standing to a different density, according to the size of its fruit, with colours to match. By January, the ranks of apples have been thinned by calls to the kitchen. The survivors are mainly a mixture of long-lasting eaters (D'Arcy Spice russets) and cookers (Bramleys and Annie Elizabeths). These will last until March. Other varieties, such as Lord Derby and Lord Suffield, have already made their way indoors to be baked into tarts, stewed puddings and pies.

Beneath the rows of waxy apples and softening Conference pears are stores of root crops. Potatoes lie buried in straw or packed loosely into old hessian sacks, while sugary carrots are hidden in large old galvanized buckets of sand. Above these, a few cabbages hang by garden twine from nails in the woodwork. All these foods, kept in the cool, dark interior of the apple store, will last for months. Eating them is sometimes a learning experience. Like meat that has been hung for weeks, the fruit and vegetables that come out of the apple store in

January have matured, gaining flavour and metabolites. A Bramley picked from the carefully ordered ranks in the store in the new year is a deeply scented, waxy object – very different from the fruit that was plucked from the tree in September or October.

As a child, I found this dimly-lit place both frightening and welcoming. Its quietness and remoteness (together with a hard-to-reach nail for the door key) meant that it was not a place you could escape from in a hurry when imaginary shadows rustled and shifted at the far end of the store (usually a mouse or, very rarely, a rat). Yet in the coldest weather, when the air outside nipped at the ends of one's nose and ears, the apple store became a refuge – a place of relative warmth, its gloomy air filled with the smell of ripening apples and dormant onions. Years later, I still find a fascination with its sleepy contents. In particular, a shock at how hard and lacking in flavour many bought apples have become; and how much fruit we waste through thinking it has begun to go rotten, when in fact it is only half ripe. Most apples now have no opportunity to become soft, wrinkled, richly scented and waxy. My guess is that in eating unripe fruit, we also miss out on some interesting micro-nutrients.

But amid the sleepy, dead or dull days of January, it is easy to forget that the seasons are still rolling on. In her words for this month, Tessa referred to the poem *Thaw* by Edward Thomas:

> *Over the land freckled with snow half-thawed*
> *The speculating rooks at their nests cawed*
> *And saw from the elm tops, delicate as flower of grass,*
> *What we below could not see, Winter pass.*

If December plumbs the true depths of winter, then January marks a gathering return to the shallows. The weather may be brutally dull or harsh at times, but amid the fog, frosts and winds, things are on the move. Underground, plants are stirring. As the tide of longer days rolls in, the first shoots of the year begin to break the surface of the earth. Behind a box hedge in the garden and in deep leaf litter in the shrubberies, yolk-yellow stars of aconites and slender green lances of snowdrop leaves push upwards. Elsewhere, on a south-west facing wall of the main house, a Winter Sweet or *Chimonanthus* breaks bud. On warm days, the air around it becomes thick with the sweet fragrance of its delicate flowers. A cut twig or branch is uplifting when taken indoors – a sign that spring, though still far off, is on the horizon.

Onion Gruel

Caroline Cranbrook/Ted Cobbin

This ancient Suffolk remedy was traditionally used to ward off colds or flu. When I first came to Great Glemham in 1970, it was recommended to me by Ted Cobbin, our old horseman, shepherd and one-time farm foreman. (His brother Edwin was employed as Backhouse Boy in the 1930s and told us that 25 staff used to sit down to mid-day meals in the servant's hall.) It is very comforting and, if diluted with additional milk or stock, makes an excellent simple soup.

1 or 2 medium-sized sliced or chopped onions
30g butter
500ml of milk
1 or 2 tablespoons of oatmeal (optional)
Ground black pepper
Salt
Grated nutmeg

Stew chopped onions in butter until semi-transparent. Add milk, oatmeal and seasonings. Simmer for five to ten minutes until the onions and oatmeal are completely soft. It is then ready to serve.

Slow-roasted Mutton Shoulder

Gerard King

True mutton is a sheep that is at least two years old or more at slaughter. Genuine, good quality mutton is pretty hard to find, particularly in this fast, fast world, but it's currently undergoing a welcome resurgence. Once cooked, mutton has a rich flavour and is more robust than lamb (which is between four to nine months old at slaughter). It is perfect for long, slow cooking. The great advantage of this recipe is its flexibility: the mutton is done when you want it to be. As long as the oven is not too hot, you can't go wrong.

1 large shoulder of mutton with the neck fillet still attached
2 garlic heads cut in half
2 or 3 peeled and halved onions
¼ litre or so of red wine
6 anchovy fillets
1 teaspoonful of chilli flakes (optional)
A bunch of fresh rosemary and thyme
Plenty of sea salt and black pepper
A large handful of roughly chopped vegetables (carrot, beetroot, parsnip)

Place the mutton in a large bowl or plastic bag and add the garlic, wine, anchovies, chilli flakes, rosemary, thyme, salt and pepper. Leave to marinade overnight. Early the next

Berbage

Caroline Cranbrook/Aileen Meade

morning, take a large oven dish. Fill the bottom with the chopped vegetables and then empty the meat and marinade over them. Tuck the garlic under the meat to avoid it burning. Sprinkle some olive oil over the meat and add a cup of water and a glass of red wine. Place a small square of foil over the meat and put in the oven for five to six hours at 130/140 C. Take off the foil for the last 40 minutes or so and turn up the oven. This gives a lovely crusty outer layer. I sometimes do this last bit out on the barbecue. Leave to stand for at least half an hour and then serve with mashed potatoes and the roasted vegetables.

This recipe for Berbage pudding came from my grandmother Aileen Meade's cookery book, but it probably originated with Lady Jekyll's *Kitchen Essays*. Suet puddings are seldom eaten nowadays, but this is one of the lighter ones and very good indeed.

110g chopped suet (Atora will do)
110g breadcrumbs
110g moist brown sugar
½ teaspoon of bicarbonate of soda
A pinch of salt
1 egg
3 heaped tablespoons of strawberry jam
Additional strawberry jam to use as a sauce

Mix all the ingredients together. Put in a pudding basin, three quarters full, and cover with grease-proof paper. Steam in a covered double-boiler for four hours. Remove and cool slightly, allowing pudding to shrink away a little from the sides of the bowl. Turn out on to a serving plate. Pour over the pudding a syrup made from warmed strawberry jam.

February

A flock of long-tailed tits on the bird feeder;
A flight of spoons, their tails not touching.

Two men huddle amongst the tools, fuelling themselves with sandwiches.
A little piece of home in an outside world.

And all around in the woods, not snow now,
But hundreds of snowdrops, silently with closed heads, keeping guard.

Tessa Newcomb

This page: Couple

February

Garden Notes

Clean leaves of citruses in greenhouses. Clean seed trays and propagators. Prick out winter lettuces in chilli house. Put warm water in frozen water drinkers for chickens. Break ice in water trough for geese. Plant new raspberry canes and label. Set up pea cage. Cut back suckers on Gallica roses. Dig up leeks. Take logs into the house and farm office. Dig sprout and cabbage bed. Set mice traps in apple store. Sow sweet peas and broad beans. Trim edges of paths in the garden. Complete rose pruning around house and garden. Water young lettuces in chilli house. Take potatoes, leeks, kale and sprouts into the house. Feed citruses in the peach house. Plant garlic. Order new mower blades. Service garden machinery – hedge trimmer, rotavator, strimmer, mower. Oil and clean tools. Check propagators.

THE POTTING SHED, like the apple store, is a long thin room tucked against the north side of the garden walls. Its entrance door is painted in Buckingham Green and is set in a wall of loosely hung wooden panelling. The whole construction rattles when the door is opened in a hurry, or slammed shut by an errant gust of north-easterly wind. Inside on the left, a tall home-made chest of drawers stands. Just as the clay uplands on which the garden stands have been fashioned by the passage of ice and water, the paths and floors within the kitchen garden have been worn down by the daily routines of the people who work there. As the decades pass, the patterns of activity shift as new machinery or gadgets arrive, poultry come and go and plants are rotated around the vegetable beds. New paths emerge and others stand abandoned or fade back into the land. The concave steps that lead down into a subterranean boiler house lie undisturbed by humans. Damp and

moss-covered, they are a home to toads, mice and newts. On the other side of the tall garden wall, the path to a dismantled conservatory has been absorbed by a thick mat of mown grass. But a hundred yards away, a new path has emerged. It leads past the potting shed and apple store to the gardener's bothy, now revived as a small studio and retreat. A narrow muddy line of trodden turf and soil flows like a small tributary to the larger marl-covered path that joins the potting shed and barrow store to the stable yard and car park beyond.

Back inside the potting shed, the front of the awkward chest of drawers is festooned with loops of sash cord. Slung between holes drilled through the front of each drawer, these serve as handles. They look like loose rigging. Some drawers are jammed tight from infrequent use. Others, in particular a shallow drawer full of shears, pruners and bill hooks, are used so often that they almost empty themselves on to the floor when their rope handles are pulled. Other furniture in the potting shed is sparse. Two old kitchen chairs stand a few yards beyond the chest, one with its back missing. A table at the back on the right is buried under old fruit nets and folded sacks. The walls of the shed are all thickly white-washed. On the left side an array of well-oiled spades, forks, hoes, edging tools, rakes, shovels, pitchforks, bow saws and other large or long-handled tools hang from large nails banged into the masonry. Opposite these, on the right side of the entrance, a battered worktop runs along more than half the length of the room. Its far end disappears into the gloom, where it runs up against the table of fruit nets and a huge pile of hardly used tins, buckets, earthenware pots, cotton netting and old sieves. On the far wall, faintly illuminated by a cobweb-festooned window, are less familiar tools. Some are veterans of another age: two-handled saws with deep-set two-pronged teeth as long as a thumb knuckle; large heavy-headed iron dibbles for planting beans; sack hooks; turf spades with long angular shafts (in profile, they look like herons' necks); and strange-looking canvas pouches for sowing seeds. Every surface is used – even the ceiling, from which hang mole traps, baskets and rolls of sacking. Half-hidden by bundles of drainage rods and sieves lurks a large hand-turned grindstone, its sandstone wheel sharply chamfered from years of lop-sided use. Like a small section of Benhall parish that has been abandoned to Great Glemham by the modern route of the River Alde, the knife grinder stands in a small oxbow of disused but heavily worn floor. Over recent decades, activity in the potting shed has moved nearer the entrance, opposite the neatly hung tools. A section of the work bench at this point is always kept tidy for potting, trimming, measuring, cutting and planning – and making tea. A large wipe board laid to one side shows a map of all the vegetables in the garden for the current year. Nearby is the gardener's diary – the source of the "Garden Notes" in each chapter. Beneath the worktop, ingrained with earth and scarred by knife blades, are two open-fronted wooden bins for leaf mould and loam. The latter is collected during the winter months from molehills on the Linen Ground – a nearby part of the park that was once used for drying laundry.

If you look around the potting shed and other parts of the garden, almost every tool and every surface has patches that are polished and worn. I remember the Suffolk poet Herbert Lomas talking about the quality an object gains through being used and touched. It can bring a richness that is hard to describe: a warmth and familiarity. The resistance of modern materials and buildings to wear and tear has many advantages. (Although, oddly, many modern objects also seem to break very easily.) But at the same time, in denying the effects of use and time, we can also lose contact with both our surroundings and our past. Both knowledge and understanding can slip from our grasp, like sand running through fingers. Some of the tools in the potting shed, besides bearing the patina of long use, also have more deliberate marks burned, etched or stamped into them. Among them are some that have been branded with the letters "CC".

This was the mark of Charles Chandler, gardener at Great Glemham House in the 1980s and 1990s. Born and bred in the village, Charlie worked in timber haulage in the 1930s and then as a commercial lorry driver later in his life, before taking on the management of the garden. He was born in Potash Cottage, at the south-west end of the parish. I remember him describing the pastures behind his parents' house being first white with field mushrooms and later pink with orchids each year; and pedalling back from the dentist in the early 1940s with a "Doodlebug" flying bomb chugging to a halt over his left shoulder. He dived off his bike as the bomb landed in a field nearby. My grandfather explored the crater the next day, taking soil samples from layers of earth never normally seen: top soil, boulder clay, sands and deeper layers of ancient alluvial deposits. It still leaves a shadow in cereal crops today.

Interviewed in the 1980s by BBC Radio Suffolk for "Down Your Way", Charlie perplexed the presenter by saying that he had no desire to leave the village nor see the rest of the world: he had left the county a few times as a haulier; had last travelled on a train in 1947; and had once made a trip to London, but found it too busy and noisy. When pressed further, he said that he was more than happy at home. His main wish was to stay and see out his days in Great Glemham. The CC-scorched handles in the potting shed survive as a testimony both to his rootedness and his knowledge about gardening, which was exceptional. He knew how to trench or double-dig, which vegetables "got on" with each other and which sequences or rotations of vegetables would not work. Charlie fulfilled his dream and saw out his time at Great Glemham. He died in his sleep in 1998. When the

Below: A little piece of home

undertakers came to carry him "home", the stable yard clock malfunctioned and played him out with an endless peal of electronic chimes. A young oak tree grows in his memory in the park.

Some of Charlie's knowledge was inherited, but much was born of experience. A deep working knowledge of soils, plants and the subtleties of the seasons is a rare currency these days – and often grossly undervalued. But it is becoming more important with the resurgent interest in allotments, market gardening and home-grown food. As the Transition Movement spreads, such knowledge is likely to become of even greater practical use. Back in the garden, conversations in February with Charlie would often turn to the weather, prompting memories of 1947. This year is still legendary in Suffolk for the coldness of its winter. The entire landscape – farm, woodland, garden, heath and even the Alde at Iken – was frozen for months on end. The beet harvest was not lifted until the following spring. Ploughing was impossible. Farms stood still and men waited to return to work on the land. My own 1947 was the more modest winter of 1986, which brought a vast but short-lived blanket of snow to East Suffolk. It was the first time I had heard true silence. A deep muffled quietness lay upon the land. There was no traffic. The only sounds were of people, dogs, birds, farm animals, church bells and the occasional plane overhead.

The winter of 1986 was overtaken more recently by the long cold spells of 2009 and 2010. These both left the garden's box hedges capped for weeks with a thick crust of re-frozen snow. Paths running between them were reduced to narrow bob sleigh runs by the daily routines of feeding the chickens, fetching foods from the apple store and checking the pelargoniums. Melt water trapped in the creases of kale leaves froze into crystal pearls at night. The air was crisp, shadows clear-cut. Such scenes have great beauty, but after more than a few days of intense cold in February, it is impossible not to be struck by the desperate plight of small mammals and birds. More than three or four inches of snow means that there is almost nothing to eat – the leaf litter, dormant shoots and warm bolt-holes in the woods are all buried and inaccessible. The animals are cut off from their food supply. The urgency of their situation is revealed by the appearance of myriad tracks in the snow around the edges of the walled garden. Rabbits, foxes, hares, pheasants, blackbirds, fieldfares, redwings and thrushes all leave distinctive trails. In the shrubberies and under the old apple trees, the last frozen remains of rotted windfalls lure blackbirds from miles around. In their hunger, they forget all rivalries and territoriality. Inside the kitchen garden, robins and thrushes join the blackbirds to poke holes in the snow underneath the box hedges. Once they have broken through, they scatter black soil and leaf litter into the icy runnels as they forage for invertebrate food.

But sooner or later comes the last thaw of winter. As the snow and ice retreat - and the demographic statistics of snowmen in Britain crash cataclysmically - life re-emerges. In the gardens, grassy paths by the vegetable beds and behind the rugosa roses look sick, bleached of colour. Where people have walked over the lawns during heavy frosts, their footprints survive as yellow scorch marks. Elsewhere in the shrubberies and on the parkland, long grass lies tousled and dishevelled, like the hair of someone who has survived the final sweat of a fever. Cultivated ground, be it a ploughed field or the vegetable beds inside the garden walls, appears puffed up and fluffy from the freezing action of heavy frosts. For a day or two, in the absence of rain or heavy dew, the delicate imprints of ice crystals may linger in the fine mud at the bottom of dry puddles. But soon, amid the gathering warmth of spring, these last signs also slip away. Julie Paternoster, who single-handedly managed the kitchen garden in the mid-1970s, once quoted Richard Jeffries and "the long-drawn breath of the land". She wrote this in a letter she kindly sent to me after my first exhibition as a painter – a collection of mud paintings from the Alde estuary and the Ashdown Forest (shown in 1994 at the Aldeburgh Cinema Gallery, then managed by Stephen Reiss). As I look back, her words have added meaning. A final thaw in February can feel like the last long exhalation of winter, before the strong in-breath of spring.

Caldo Verde
Caroline Cranbrook

A simple Portuguese soup, delicious hot or cold. It is quick and easy to make and the water in which the potatoes and greens are cooked is not wasted. Kale is such a useful and versatile vegetable, always there in the coldest winter months and very attractive too. Like most brassicas, kales are much improved by being sweated in hot butter or olive oil after cooking and they tend to taste sweeter as the weather gets colder, so January and February are good months to eat these winter greens.

450g potatoes
1 small chopped onion
1 chopped garlic clove
1 tablespoon of olive oil
A large handful of chopped greens (kale, cabbage, spinach)
Ground black pepper
Sea salt
1.25 - 1.75l of water

Put all the ingredients, except the kale, into a saucepan and boil until the potatoes are soft. Mash and bring back to the boil. Add finely chopped kale or other greens and boil for a couple more minutes. Liquidise further if the greens are too large or seaweed-like for your taste.

Wood Pigeon Sausage Rolls
Peter Harrison

Butchers and our local Wild Meat Company usually have pigeons for sale. They can be roasted whole but generally only the breasts are used. This recipe provides a tasty portable snack or can be served on a bed of braised red cabbage and lentils.

400g of free-range pork sausage meat
6 pigeon breasts
A single 6cm x 10cm square of puff pastry
A sprig of thyme
A pinch each of ground mace and cayenne
Salt & pepper
Zest of one orange
Egg-wash (lightly beaten raw egg)

Preheat the oven to 180C. Seal pigeon breasts in a hot pan on both sides, then set them aside. Mix the thyme, mace, cayenne, salt, pepper and orange zest into the sausage meat. Divide the sausage meat mixture into six portions and wrap a portion round each of the pigeon breasts. Brush egg wash over each of the pastry squares and place a pigeon/sausage meat portion centrally on to each square. Roll up each portion into a "sausage roll" shape and brush a little more egg wash over the top. Place the rolls on a baking tray and bake for about fifteen minutes at 180C until golden brown. Serve hot.

Leek & Potato Gratin

Claire Bruce-Clayton

This is one of those satisfying, heart-warming dishes which is perfect for supper on a cold night or to return to after a brisk winter walk. The following recipe will feed six hungry people.

6 large main crop potatoes
4 or 5 large leeks
A good wedge of Stilton
2 generous handfuls of shelled walnuts
150g of butter
1 mug of breadcrumbs

Peel the potatoes, slice thickly and boil for eight to ten minutes, so that they are tender, but still holding their shape. Drain them. While the potatoes are cooking, wash, slice and sauté the leeks with butter and seasoning until tender. Butter a baking dish, cover the bottom with a layer of potato slices, then a layer of leeks, walnuts and some crumbled blue cheese. Repeat the layers, lightly seasoning each of them. Finish with the cheese and scatter breadcrumbs over the top. Cook in a medium (180C) oven for 20-30 minutes until the cheese is melted and bubbling. I love the crunch of the walnuts in this dish, but if you wish you can add a few chopped and sautéed rashers of streaky bacon instead.

Baked Apples

Caroline Cranbrook

Baked apples are a good standby in the winter. This recipe helps to use up the last apples from the apple store. Bramleys or Annie Elizabeth, a 19th century variety, both work well. Annie Elizabeth is quite sweet for a cooker, maintains its shape during cooking and keeps for months if stored in a dark cool place.

6 apples
Dried fruit (eg, raisins, chopped dates)
50g of brown sugar
Butter
Powdered/ground cinnamon
2 or 3 tablespoons of water

Core apples and cut a thin line round the outside of the middle with a sharp knife – this stops the apple from exploding. Stuff the hollow core with the dried fruit, topping it with a smear of butter, a teaspoon of brown sugar and a pinch of ground cinnamon. Place in a baking dish with a little water and cook for up to an hour at 180C. Check from time to time with a skewer. They will be done when the skin can be pierced easily and there is no internal resistance to the point. Serve with fresh cream, crème fraiche or ice cream.

March

The walnut tree was there – now just
a stump but around it these new shoots –
I wanted to tell someone.

The Spangled Hamburg drinks water.
Tidy little lady amongst this rampant
social life.

Everything's blown clean. The wind's keen. This year March is going out
like a lion. Hear it roar outside the walls.

Tessa Newcomb

This page: Brown hare

March

Garden Notes

Finish assembling pea cage. Pollinate apricot and peach blossom in the peach house. Tie up vines. Hoe weeds on ploughed vegetable beds. Tidy the sheds. Stand out seed potatoes. Deliver leeks, store potatoes and kale to the house. Re-fit covers and bird scare twine to cabbages and broccoli. Fix wire to pea cage. Take winter cover off the olive tree. Weed garden paths. Cut hazel tops for pea sticks from woods and shrubberies. Prick out cabbages. Tidy wood store. Clean and feed chrysanthemums. Prepare ground and plant early potatoes (Belle de Fontenay, Cherie, Foremost). Sow seeds and prick out seedlings into pots. Start mowing lawns.

MARCH SEES THE FINAL emptying of the apple store. What has not been eaten in the house or delivered to local pubs and cafés is fed to the chickens or scattered in the shrubberies for wild birds. The potting shed, which has been a refuge during the winter months, opens its doors to the garden and greenhouses once again. Seeds are sown, pricked out, potted and transplanted. Trays for seedlings are filled with compost and the rich molehill soil stored in the potting shed. Canes previously cut from a large clump of bamboo growing on a west facing lawn are taken down from the rafters of the barrow store. Once cleaned, they are set out in neat lines among the broccoli, kales and cabbages. By the end of March the garden will be bursting with young shoots. In the meantime it is essential to start warding off predators, especially pigeons, which have an immense appetite for spring greens. A flat twine or tape is tied tightly between the canes now standing amid the brassicas, criss-crossing the patch like a huge game of cats' cradle. When a breeze blows in, the taut twine vibrates, emitting a loud zooming hum. I remember once visiting a demonstration of Maori music at a community hall or marae on Waiheke Island in New Zealand – the sound of the twine is very like that of small Maori wind-blade instruments called *purerehua*. On windy days the lattice of twine works perfectly, repelling pigeons and other birds. But on calm days, it stands mute and ineffective, like an unplucked harp.

Other structures begin to appear as March progresses. Timber and old scaffolding pipes are nailed and wired together in one quarter of the garden to create a large pea cage. Once the framework has been assembled, a big roll of galvanized chicken wire is carefully unwound around it and bundles of green plastic netting spread out over the top. The seams between wire and netting are sewn up with string and short snippets of bailer twine. The final piece of the jigsaw is a small door hung from ancient hinges nailed into a rickety frame of old boards. The making of the cage is an elaborate process, but without it there would be no peas to pick later in the year.

The bird scaring twine and the pea cage are both seasonal structures. They are also nomadic, moving from one part of the garden to another as the crops that they protect rotate around the four main vegetable patches. Some of the other structures that offer protection to plants are more permanent. In the north-east quarter of the garden, a large fruit cage covers almost a third of an acre. Sheltered within it are rows of currants, raspberries and gooseberry bushes, bordered on one side by two lines of espaliered apple and pear trees. Each plant is pruned during the winter and receives a good dose of wood-ash to boost its annual supply of potash. After that, they are left to bud and blossom in the permanent safety of the cage. Occasionally, a blackbird slips inside looking for food. In March this does not matter too much – it may find a few worms to pull in the grassy leaf litter beneath the apple and pear trees, but not much else. In June, July and August it will discover a feast of currants, gooseberries and raspberries.

The most robust of all the structures inside the walls of the garden are four greenhouses. Three of them were originally built in the early 1820s. Two were built side by side but "on the huh" (local dialect, meaning "on the slant" – see Appendix IV). Of these, the main frame of one has survived – now fitted with large Perspex panels. The other was rebuilt from the brickwork upwards

Below: Lions and lambs

in the 1990s. A third, separated from the first two greenhouses by the main entrance to the garden, was rebuilt in the second half of the 19th century. The main frames of the first two greenhouses were made of oak set on red brick footings. They were fitted with eight pairs of sliding roof panels, each glazed with almost one hundred lapped panes of glass – all cut at a slight angle to form rhomboid panes. We have often wondered if there was some subtle reason for this, but my guess is that the designer or builder made a mistake and it was cheaper to carry on. Almost two hundred years later, when the balance in the value of materials and people's time has changed, the awkward angles lead to some high maintenance costs.

The first greenhouse is now known as "the chilli house". A solitary goldfish lives in its water tank and the interior is planted each year with my mother's favourite varieties of chillies, basil, aubergines and peppers. Lablab beans sprawl up wire trelliswork, spilling stalks of rich purple blossom later in the year. The second greenhouse has become "the peach house" and is home to an apricot, nectarine and peach tree, together with three citruses – a lemon, lime and blood orange. These grow in raised brick-faced beds along the inside front wall of the greenhouse. Subterranean arches along the external wall give their roots access to a feeder bed outside. The floor of the peach house is part bare earth and part tiled. A wide culvert covered with elaborately decorated ironwork conceals redundant heating pipes. These wind their way under all the greenhouses. They were once connected to a large boiler, but this ceased functioning decades ago. It was housed in a small room beyond the barrow store. When I was a child a large cavity in the floor marked the place from which it had been extracted, like an old molar tooth. The hole has since been filled in with concrete and the room doubles up as a workshop.

The third greenhouse is the vine house. The basic arrangement of footings and floor is the same as in the chilli house and peach house, but the original woodwork has been replaced with a more open design and much larger (and straighter) glazing panels. It was rebuilt in the 19th century and again in 2010. Instead of sliding sashes it has four articulated roof lights that are raised and lowered by an elegant arrangement of iron levers on the inner wall. The individual panes of glass on the roof are all also cut with a curved lower edge, which encourages rain water to run down the middle of the panes, rather than the edges (which rapidly rots the main frame). It is a small detail, but its thoughtfulness is symbolic of many other Regency and Victorian design features in the garden which work quietly with the elements and natural forces.

The vines are a mixture of black Hamburgs, white Muscats (several as old as the house) and some much younger strawberry grapes. Again, there is a feeder bed in front of the vine house and a collection of large iron heating pipes inside. In the vine house, the pipes are exposed, running around the front of the raised bed in which the grape vines grow. At one end, there is a flat pad where two large pipes merge into one. A small brass steam release valve with a turn-screw is mounted on the top of the join. As a child, no more than four or five years old, I remember playing steam trains. This involved sitting on the pad and twiddling the brass turn-screw, imagining that the iron pipes that curved around the interior of the greenhouse were somehow the engine's barrel-like boiler and the valve was the chimney. Four decades later, the valve still twiddles around, but the pad seems miniscule, reaching no higher than my shin.

The last greenhouse is a modern aluminium structure, built on the footprint of an old cucumber forcing house. Its new metal frame will never rot and the maintenance costs are a fraction of those for the other greenhouses. Inside, a network of raised brickwork beds are underlain by more iron heating pipes. In March the beds are home to my mother's collection of pelargoniums, potted primulas, and a large tropical lime tree. Brought back as a seedling from Malaysia in 1970, the lime has never flowered, but its richly scented leaves are an excellent spice for fresh fish and green curries. The primulas include a dozen or so potted specimens of the wild form of *Primula malacoides* (the Fairy Primula). These were salvaged from the ruins of the original peach house by my mother and George Smith in the early 1970s, where they were growing amid the collapsed remains of wooden staging. They are beautiful, delicate flowers. My mother thinks that they may have been brought back as seed from Tibet or Upper Burma by my grandfather Jock Cranbrook in 1931. Soon, as the pelargoniums move to the stable yard and the primulas go into the house, the beds in the greenhouse will be taken over by young aubergines and chillies. Set amid the brickwork of the raised beds is an old galvanized metal water tank, its folded seams sealed by lines of rivets. It is a small oasis, fed by a stand pipe capped with a well-worn brass tap. Watering cans rest nearby, ready for use. The insides of the tank are lined with a forest of water weed. At night, flatworms come out to graze, wandering underneath the water's surface. They have lived in the tank for more than 40 years. As a child, I watched them coast around in their upside-down world. It was one of the perks of shutting up the chickens at night, armed with a large torch.

My mother has provided a list of garden "pests" that can be a nuisance in the confines of the walled garden: mice, rats, voles, moles, squirrels, pigeons, pheasants, partridges, slugs, snails, caterpillars, nematodes, wasps, red spider, whitefly, greenfly, blackfly, potato blight, tomato blight, honey fungus and botrytis. I was happy in my writing to focus on the productivity and the design of the gardens at Glemham in which Tessa has been working, but my mother was keen to also emphasise that gardening can at times be a battle – mainly because this is so often not mentioned in gardening makeover programmes on TV or in magazines. Growing food at home or in allotments and market gardens can be a vital and very fulfilling process, but it can be hard or demoralising work if you are not ready for the problems that may lie in wait. Of the pests listed, most of the larger animals can be warded off by netting and walls, or simply the presence of someone working in the garden. Mice and rats in store rooms need trapping and removing. Fungal infections – particularly mildews and blight – need instant attention. There is no greater tragedy in vegetable gardening than seeing row after row of potatoes and heavily laden tomato plants turn black, wither and die from blight. In addition to these challenges, weed seeds are also ready in the wings, waiting to make the most of the fertile soil.

Well-manured and well-dug earth can help reduce the risk of infestations or infections. A deep, rich, well-drained and well-aerated soil is the foundation of a good garden. Mixed cropping and careful rotations can also help maintain plant health. But a good working knowledge of how to protect vegetables and fruits from predation and disease is also vital.

In response to the ravages of gastropods in the garden, Alan Sharpe (2001-2005) trimmed part of an old length of box hedge into a huge slug and a matching snail, complete with eye stalks. Whether they have a deterrent effect or serve as a totem is not clear, but they have become a feature of the garden. In some cases, food plants are still able to defend themselves with thorns or cocktails of chemicals. But most commonly grown fruits and vegetables – like cows, sheep, goats and pigs – have been rendered palatable and harmless by centuries or even millenia of domestication. I remember Peter Lanyon, a biology teacher at my secondary school, explaining that most plants do not want to be eaten. The flesh of fruits are "deliberate" offers or concessions to animals. In return for eating the palatable flesh, animals become dispersal agents, depositing seeds far from their parents and sometimes even in convenient piles of nutritious manure. But in the wild, shoots, roots and growing tips are often protected in some way. It has taken generations of careful seed collection and selective breeding to make our lettuces, cabbages, broccolis and many other vegetables so harmless and palatable.

Some plants in the garden still retain partial toxicity. Further round the outer gravel path from Alan's leafy gastropods, beyond an ailing Lord Derby apple tree, a self-sown walnut has been felled to protect the rhubarb plants beneath it. Chemicals from its fallen leaves were suppressing the rhubarb – which itself has an edible stalk, but toxic leaves. When I was growing up in the 1970s, rhubarb leaves were on a "danger list" of poisonous plants. A sense that the garden was basically safe but laced with risk was heightened by other hazards. Some were clearly identified, but others were more nebulous: yew tree berries; the deep water butts in front of the greenhouses (all concealed beneath wire covers); a swampy pond in the shrubberies; and a tarred shed by Charlie Chandler's vegetable patch. The last of these concealed the ultimate horror – a well. The fact that it was sealed up did not matter. It lurked within the harmless wooden shed: locked up, deep and dangerous!

These terrors all shrank as years passed. Nobody swallowed any yew berries; the water butts stayed safe; the swampy pond has been restored to its former glory (it is now clear again, full of lilies and mysterious Water Soldiers, a native of the Fens); and the well still lurks, but not so menacingly. The rhubarb patch is in full spate, released from the inhibitory effects of the walnut tree. The first sweet crimson stems are usually ready towards the end of March. The scent they release when cut is amazing – sweet, crisp and tart, even to the nose. Outside the confines of the walled garden in the shrubberies, snowdrops and aconites are already fading, giving way to the taller, leathery green blades and elegant slipper-like buds of daffodils. These bring a flush of yellow to the apple orchards and herbaceous borders. Elsewhere, older more modest varieties, including the 18th century Butter & Eggs and wild Lent Lilies, add softer colours to the woodland floor, often accompanied by the first sharp shoots of Ramsons or wild garlic.

Purple Sprouting Broccoli & Pasta

Lola de Mille

Spring sprouting broccolis are a great delicacy and should be appreciated even more than other highly seasonal vegetables. The plants take nearly a year to mature and quickly progress to a mass of sweet smelling yellow blossom, as appetising to bees as their shoots are to us. The shoots are well worth searching out in local shops and farmers' markets. They have a great depth of flavour and go well with sharp and salty ingredients.

450g purple sprouting broccoli
1 or more cloves of garlic
Chilli to taste
225g of pancetta lardons
6 sun-blushed tomatoes
Pine nuts and parmesan cheese (with quantities to your taste)

Fry the sliced garlic and chilli over a medium heat in a wok or large frying pan. Remove, turn up the heat and add the pancetta lardons. Return to the heat and fry until crisp. Then add the purple sprouting broccoli, sliced in half length-ways. Cook for a few minutes and add some sliced, sun-blushed tomatoes. Cook for one more minute. Serve with pasta, sprinkled with pine nuts and grated parmesan.

Nettles with Coriander & White Fish

Jason Gathorne-Hardy

This recipe is based on a dish I once tried in northern Spain. It is typically made with spinach, but nettles work well as a substitute. Pluck the growing tips and first pair of leaves from the stems - wear gloves! Nettle with coriander goes well with steamed or fried white fish, such as plaice, haddock or cod. In East Suffolk, inshore fishing boats operate from Lowestoft, Walberswick, Dunwich, Sizewell, Thorpeness, Aldeburgh, Orford, Bawdsey and Felixstowe.

The heads of 20 to 30 common nettle plants

Wash the nettle tips and drop them into a pan of water that is boiling hard. Leave with the lid on for four minutes. Remove pan and let it cool for a few minutes. Carefully strain off the water. Squeeze the nettle tips with a wooden spoon to press out remaining water. Place the tips in a blender. Add seasoning to your taste: coarse ground black pepper, salt, butter and cream, with a tiny bit of olive oil. Blend the mix, adding powdered coriander, again to taste. Use the vivid green sauce as an accompaniment for steamed or fried white fish.

Gorse Flower Panna Cotta

Andrew Blackburn

Gorse grows in abundance in East Suffolk on sandy soils near the coast. A piece of local folklore is that "When the gorse is in flower, it's the season for courting". Gorse bushes flower all year round: a perfect excuse for a romantic walk.

A level cupful/75gm of fresh gorse petals
300ml double cream
3 leaves of gelatine
300ml full fat milk
100g icing sugar
2 stamens of saffron

Wash and break up the fresh petals. Pour double cream into a saucepan Add gorse petals, icing sugar and saffron. Bring to simmer and continue to boil gently for another hour until cream has reduced by about one sixth. Remove pan from heat and leave the mixture to infuse for three hours. Soak the gelatine strips in the milk until soft, then add the milk and gelatine to the cream. Stir until gelatine has dissolved. Pour the infused cream through a fine sieve to strain out the flower heads. Pour the panna cotta into moulds and leave in a fridge to set.

Brown Bread Cream

Doddington Cookery Book/Caroline Cranbrook

A very simple and unusual way of eating cream. It was a favourite when I was a child at my family home in Lincolnshire. The cream came from the house Jersey cow (milked by the under- gardener) and the bread was made by the cook, Mrs Barber, from a sackful of flour which stood in a large metal-lidded barrel in a corner of the kitchen. We loved helping her and marking the cross "to let out the old witch" on the mound of dough before it was set out to rise in a large bowl on the floor in front of the Aga.

1 pint of stiffly whipped double cream, to which 2oz of fine brown bread crumbs are added, with a little sugar to taste. It goes well with almost all puddings and stewed fruit.

April

I have not been here for more than
a month. I come full of expectation.

A builder appears high on the
wall. He is replacing missing coping
bricks. His Radio One fills the gap
between the bird songs.

I go back to read the old label on the
apple tree. It's just blue.

Tessa Newcomb

This page:Bear's breeches

74

April

Garden Notes

Dig over old leek bed. Plant peas. Hoe around chard and spinach. Cut hazel and pine for Spring Festival. Dig out nettles from lavenders. Dig up and thin Day Lilies to give room for roses. Plant main crop of Desiree potatoes. Prepare veg boxes for tenants. Plant summer cauliflowers and cover with netting. Feed citruses. Water vines. Spray vines with fungicide. Trim and thin out fruit on apricot tree. Rake garden paths. Plant out young Italian artichokes. Prick out calabrese and lettuce seedlings. Cut out dead stems from soft fruit in the fruit cage. Break up last year's leek bed and summer cabbage bed with rotavator. Tie up vines. Flood peach, apricot and vines to water the roots. Start clearing winter brassicas. Easter Holidays.

IN THE MIDDLE of the walled garden there is a deep circular basin or dipping pond, previously used by gardeners to fill their watering cans. It is lined with a layer of mortar, the rim of which is capped by a ring of dressed limestone. Wrought iron railings run around the pond, supported by posts and diagonal cross-frames. Each post is crowned with a palm-sized iron bauble and its base is set into a chiselled socket plugged with lead – an old technique for fixing metal into stone. The cross frames are rusted and flaky, but the balls are smoother, worn down by passing hands. On sunny days, even in April, they become warm to the touch.

A wide gravel path runs around the pond, interrupted on the northwest side by a large sandstone slab. This looks a bit forlorn, lying slightly askew with a rough fracture across its middle. The layered break reveals a glimpse of a dark hole beneath – a brick-lined cistern that is plumbed to the Green Pond in the shrubberies. The interior of the hole, like that of the old boiler room tucked inside the southern wall of the garden, is cool and damp. It is a refuge for woodlice, newts and large brown garden snails, which gather together like land limpets in lumpy, suckered clusters. I used to heave the slab up as a child to look in wonder at the sleeping animals and piles of rich worm casts that covered the bottom of the hole. The fracture in the slab was my doing – to my embarrassment. After one afternoon's exploring, the weight of the slab was too much. Fearing for my fingers and feet, I let one end drop down. It fell into place with a resounding hollow boom and loud grating crack. I left shocked, amid echoes of guilt, but with my fingers and toes intact.

The pond is the focal point of the garden. To the north, south, east and west it opens on to long paths that lead towards the outer walls and a much larger circular path. Between the gravel-covered junctions around the pond are beds of large irises, their young leaves rising from their corms like broad powder-green knife blades. Above the flower beds a pergola of pine and metal poles encircles the whole pond, entwined with the rose American Pillar. Wizened stumps give way to younger more pliable stems above, their purple-tipped shoots beginning to stir. The paths that strike out to the east and west pass between large vegetable beds – the home of the fruit cage, pea cage, asparagus bed, artichokes and brassicas. Bordered by carefully trimmed box hedges and narrow belts of grass, they are overshadowed by broken lines of fruit trees. These include a large mulberry, an olive (which is unwrapped in March or April), two plums (Marjorie's Seedling and a new Denbigh plum), two Doyenne de Comice pears (grafted by George Smith – see Appendix I) and several apple trees (including Annie Elizabeth, Lady Henniker, D'Arcy Spice and Dr Harvey). Between them is a scattering of ivy-clad stumps – the remains of older trees that have died, knocked over by the 1987 hurricane or consumed by mistletoe. The survivors and younger grafted replacement trees begin to break bud in April, their bare crowns erupting into slowly unfolding explosions of blossom.

The two remaining paths, running from north to south, are the main visual axis of the garden. They run between a commemorative iron

gate at their southern end and a large green door at the north. This is the main work entrance to the garden. On the inside, it opens on to the vine house and peach house; outside it leads to the potting shed, barrow store and apple store. The north-south paths are much wider, fringed on both sides by broad herbaceous borders. Over the years, the level of the paths has gradually increased, like an ancient highway, as more stones are laid on top. They are slowly developing their own archaeology as layers of modern pea gravel slowly bury the last low outcrops of a much thicker layer of marl. This mixture of clay, flint and chalk was the original surface material for almost all the paths at Glemham House, both inside the kitchen garden and outside among the lawns and shrubberies. It was excavated from a pit near the Dell, the last barrow loads being dug up in the late 1980s. The hole left by this last extraction quickly became a childhood hideout, and then part of my father's fern garden. My younger brother Argus, our cousin Freddy and I all experimented with a *Stig of the Dump* existence at different times, sheltering for hours or even days beneath four sheets of rusting tin laid between the lip of the pit and a long arching root of dead elm. I armed myself with flints and sticks, constructed a fireplace out of an up-ended drain pipe and, with friends, tried growing a small patch of wheat, believing this would make us firmly

Neolithic in both outlook and character. Freddy and Argus, aged about 8, were more audacious and actually took up residence in the pit for a while, inviting our mother and a friend as guests for a feast of wild garlic and rabbit stew. I think the guests made polite and agreeable supping noises, ate little and enjoyed the meal greatly. Freddy and Argus were more committed, and probably hungrier. They ate the lot. A later experiment with not quite so well cooked rabbit left them both in bed for several days with stomach upsets.

In April, the wide beds of the north-south herbaceous borders come alive with daffodils, crocuses and hyacinths. Lupins begin to push up closed fans of lush young leaves and, at the back of the borders, lines of gallica and rugosa roses show signs of growth. On the ground the first flowers of spring seem to continue their march through the spectrum, moving from the pale whites and yellows of February and March to the

richer yellows of early April and the first bursts of pinks and blues towards the beginning of May.

Set within this gathering profusion of early spring growth, the pond itself goes through similar cycles, interrupted over the years by periods of collapse as subsidence pulls open large cracks in its mortar lining. I remember from the 1970s the occasional silver flash of rudd as they dashed for cover in dense clumps of water weed and the cream-orange bellies of newts struggling more laboriously through the tangled stems. A plank of wood propped against the rim of the pond enabled frogs and toads to leave after spawning. The first cracks in the pond appeared in the 1980s, causing it to leak slowly. It was not enough to empty it, but the water level would fall steadily if the valve in the cistern wasn't opened up – a job made easier by my accident with the stone slab. The Great Storm of 1987 rendered this action impossible.

I was away at university at the time, but my parents and sister Flora were at home. They spent the night of the storm huddled together in our parents' bedroom, after the windows of my sister's room were blown in by the sheer force of 100 mile an hour gusts of wind slamming into the south side of the house. In the darkness, above the scream and roar of the wind, they heard the great oaks of the park and woods crash like galleons, shattering into the clay and sandy soil. In the morning, they rose to find a changed landscape. More than 120 oaks, five acres of pines and 20 acres of poplar trees lay felled, broken or smashed on the ground. Remarkably, the greenhouses in the garden all survived, but in the shrubberies, a large Cedar of Lebanon lost the top fifteen feet of its trunk. This had snapped like a match and somersaulted over half a lawn. Another casualty was the original iron water pipe that fed the dipping pond. It was pulled apart by the upended root plate of a large lime tree. The tree is still alive today. It forms a large living lintel over a path, its trunk cradled in the branches of a neighbouring yew. Stripped of its original water supply, the dipping pond, recently re-sealed by Chris Ellis, now has to be filled by hosepipes and the rain.

Looking at the arrangement of paths, pond, greenhouses and entrances to the kitchen garden, it is clear that a principal aim of the

design was to enable the owners of the house and their guests to walk into the garden without having to get too close to the hard graft of production. The view from the central path is, to be fair, enchanting, as I am sure was intended. Later in the year, broad swathes of lupins, daisies, sweet williams and irises are backed by rows of scented roses, beyond which one gets fleeting glimpses of the vegetable beds, fruit trees and carefully trimmed box hedges. But today the strict social barriers and hierarchies that prevailed when the house, park and garden were created no longer exist. The kitchens, laundry and staff accommodation are now people's homes. The garden is more equal and also more communal. Family and friends gather produce; students from local primary schools and the charity East Feast occasionally come to visit; and residents have their own patches or "plats". The plot of land that Charlie Chandler once cultivated now supports artichokes. A longer strip around the edge of the garden is tended by Bill and Maureen Philpot, who live in one of the flats next to the Stable Yard.

It is encouraging to see that the garden has survived through significant social changes – sometimes upheavals - without ceasing production. After World War II, many country houses were wholly or partly demolished or their gardens lost. Glemham House was fortunate to avoid this end and has pulled through, losing only a conservatory, the old gasworks, a small museum and the garden boilers. The number of people working in the garden has dropped dramatically – from five or six in the 1930s to one full time gardener today. Like his predecessors, Chris Ellis has been supported by other employees who have worked on the family farms all their adult lives: Anthony Heffer (former ploughman and part-time gamekeeper – who featured in Ronald Blythe's *Akenfield*); Michael Salter (ex farm foreman); Ronnie Watling (former estate maintenance man and builder). With their help over the years and the efforts of my grandparents and parents the garden has continued to produce food not just for our own family but for friends, neighbours and, more recently, a small but growing number of chefs and food businesses in the area – notably Lawsons Delicatessen in Aldeburgh and Café 1885 at Snape Maltings. The garden also supplies the annual Alde Valley Spring Festival, which opens in mid April at White House Farm a few hundred yards away in the bottom of the Upper Alde Valley.

Education is also coming into the garden. Small Knowledge Fairs* at recent Alde Valley Spring Festivals highlighted the resurgent interest in gardening as a means of providing food for individuals, families and communities. This seems to be a global phenomenon and I can see a stage at which forms of expanded gardening may begin to replace conventional agriculture as a dominant source of food for communities around the world, re-uniting people with the earth and soils at our feet. My hope is that the gardens at Great Glemham will find a role to play in this transition.

* The Alde Valley Knowledge Fairs take their inspiration from the biennial E-Bario community Knowledge Fairs started in the Kelabit Highlands of Sarawak in 2007. www.ebario.com

St George's Mushroom Omelette

Claire Bruce-Clayton

St George's Day mushrooms start to appear near to the saint's day on 23rd April. They grow in rings in ancient pasture or often in woodland. They dry well and keep their flavour for up to a year.

450g St George's mushrooms
Eggs (2 per person)
Butter
Seasoning

When trimmed and cleaned, cut them into quarters or halves and put them in a pan with heated butter and seasoning. Keep the heat low so that they cook through without drying out. For the omelette, use a couple of good-sized eggs per person. Break into a bowl, add seasoning and a dash of cold water. Whisk the eggs gently with a fork. Heat up the pan, add a knob of butter and, when it is foaming, pour in your eggs. Draw the cooked curds into the centre, tilting your pan from time to time until the omelette is still creamy on top but set. Scatter over the cooked mushrooms, fold the omelette and flip on to a plate. Eat with a simple green salad. Try mixing red mustard leaves, mizuna and chicory leaves with purslane, which has a great crunchy texture.

Sicilian Cauliflower Salad

Caroline Cranbrook

Cooked cauliflower can be the dullest or the most delicious of vegetables. The vegetable has a long history. Thought to be native to Italy, it was known to the Romans but was only widely introduced to European cuisine in the 16th century. At the court of Louis XIV it is even described as a delicacy. In the kitchen garden we grow three varieties: the standard white Snowball, the acid green Marzatico and the purple Violetta di Sicilia, whose colour is derived from the anti-oxidant anthocyanins it contains (likewise in red cabbage or blood oranges). Here is a Sicilian recipe.

3 small cauliflower heads (1 white, 1
*   green, 1 purple – but 3 white will do)*
6 minced anchovies
2 medium-sized red peppers
15 to 20 black olives
5 tablespoons of olive oil
Juice of 1 large lemon
Freshly ground black pepper
Salt
Fresh parsley

Roast the peppers in the oven at 230 C for fifteen minutes and until they are blackened on one side. Turn over and roast for a further fifteen minutes. Remove, put in a covered bowl until cool; then peel and deseed. Divide the cauliflower heads into florets and blanch for several minutes in boiling water, removing before they become soggy. (The shorter the period of blanching, the more the purple and green cauliflowers retain their colour.) Drain and plunge into cold water. When they have cooled, remove, pat dry and mix immediately with the chopped peppers, anchovies and black olives, followed by olive oil and lemon juice beaten together with the seasonings. Add the freshly chopped herbs (eg, parsley, tips of winter savory) and refrigerate before serving.

Roast Muntjac in a Cream Sauce
Freddy Gathorne-Hardy

Muntjac deer are quite small but delicious.

1 saddle of muntjac on the bone
3 cloves of garlic
A small glass of brandy
Red currant or other fruit jelly
Cooking oil
Salt
Black pepper
150ml cream

Heat oven to 230C. Crush garlic and rub it into the meat with salt and pepper. In a baking tray heat two tablespoons of oil over a hot hob. Sear and brown the meat on all sides on top of the stove and then put into the hot oven. Roast for about fifteen minutes (plus five minutes if you like it well-cooked). Remove, cover and leave to rest for fifteen minutes in a warm place. Next, pour a glass of brandy over the meat and return it in its tray to the hob and heat until the brandy and juice are warm and the brandy burnt off. Remove the meat and put on a warm serving dish. Deglaze the tray and add a spoonful of jelly. When melted, stir in the cream. As soon as this boils remove from the heat. Serve in thick slices with potatoes and the sauce poured over the whole.

May

*I open the gate and am greeted by Annie
Elizabeth. The bare blue label tree
now wears a party dress of blossom as
if to say "Look at me, I can still do it!"*

The sound of a rake and loud birds.

*We've had warmth. Lots of lettuces, buttonholes
on the brown earth. Marshall – the glossiest
maroon – shiny with health.*

Tessa Newcomb

This page:Broad beans

May

Garden Notes

Dig out old cut lettuce stems and roots. Leave trickle tube watering on overnight for spinach and red beet. Trim box hedges. Water lettuces and cabbages. Sow French beans and plant last of calabrese and lettuces. Thin and trim peaches. Weed and pick over young aubergine and pepper plants in pots. Hoe paths, asparagus and other beds. Gap up summer spinach. Hoe pea cage, beans, onions, potatoes. Harvest asparagus. Dig up old Italian parsley. Prune vines. Gap up dwarf beans, courgettes and cucumbers. Cut rhubarb for the house. Lettuces and herbs for the Spring Festival. Time off for the Suffolk Show and May Bank Holidays.

THERE IS A LONG thin stretch of woodland to the north of the walled garden and shrubberies called Backhousepond Covert. One end of the wood is semi-wild, a mixture of self-sown hazel, hornbeam, willow, silver birch, oak and ash trees. The middle is full of shallow ponds, old pollarded oaks and the remains of ancient embankments, all of which suggest that this is the site of an old settlement and roadway. To one side of these discreet landscape features is a huge pit, about 80 yards wide and 150 yards long. Thousands of tons of sand subsoil were scooped out by hand and horse-drawn cart in the late 18th or early 19th centuries. Long-since unused, the pit is now home to badgers, foxes, rabbits and tall sycamore trees. The narrower western slope of the pit, covered by young nettles in early May, was used as the "backhouse" rubbish dump in the late 19th and early 20th centuries. A dark stain of rich spoil stains the underlying sand, covering a land-slip of broken crockery, old bottles and the rusted flanks of several bottomless metal buckets, their handles still attached. Some of this rubbish was probably barrowed to the pit by Edwin Cobbin, who worked as the backhouse boy between 1923 and 1926. (See Appendix I)

The southern portion of Backhousepond Covert doubles up as the boundary of the parkland around Glemham House. Its structure is that of a classic English plantation: mature "standard" oaks tower above an extensive understorey of hazel coppice. Besides providing an attractive frame for views of the parkland from both the house and a nearby lane, this combination of oak and hazel was also designed to be intensely productive over many generations. The hazel would have provided wood for thatching pegs, hurdles and sticks or canes every five to seven years. The planted oaks would have been cropped over much longer periods. The first yield would have been rounds of tall thinnings, taken after 30 or 40 years. More substantial trees would become available after 100 to 150 years of growth, producing quantities of prime timber for construction and furniture making – and bark for tanning leather. The oaks that stand in the wood today are the survivors of past thinnings. Most of them are about 200 years old. Some are dying back; others are still in full swing, with large canopies and expanding girths.

In a short foreword for A O D Claxton's book *Suffolk Dialect*, my grandfather Jock Cranbrook wrote: "Linguistics, like forestry, makes one want a double life span." Looking around the parkland and woods at Great Glemham, one can understand this desire, for the old oaks and chestnuts sail through the centuries, their stories largely untold or unknown. Each tree is an event in itself, the extraordinary aftermath of a small seed falling to earth. When trees are felled, for timber or safety reasons, their fresh stumps – especially those of ash trees – have the appearance of bright ponds into which pebbles have been dropped. Growth rings ripple out through time from the centre, the middle ring of each stump marking the precise spot at which a seed once hit the ground. Each tree stands as an echo of this tiny impact, an upward splash in time. My grandfather ended his foreword "… but nevertheless, I am glad to have seen Mr. Claxton's book in one lifetime." Perhaps it is the same with these ancient trees – it is good to have known them even for a short while, to be a passing acquaintance in their much longer life spans.

Beyond Backhousepond Covert, my own farm stretches out over pastures and flood meadows towards its eastern boundary, the River Alde. The fields are dotted with oaks, some at least 400 years old. In the parkland around the main house beside a patch of grass called the Heart – covered in pheasant's eye daffodils in May – stands what remains of The Double Oak. Two hollowed trunks used to grow up and away from each other, separated by four feet of bare earth. One half was blown over in the 1987 storm; the other survives. Oliver Rackham examined the two trunks in the early 1980s and suggested that they were the remnants of a single oak tree of "immeasurable antiquity". It is possible an oak has stood on this ground for almost a thousand years.

These ancient trees stand like ancestors or guardians, quietly ploughing on through long episodes of growth and decay as years, decades and even centuries flow by. Around them fields, boundaries, houses and whole cultures have appeared, flourished and passed. Trees that were last pollarded to provide timbers for the curved ribs of Nelson's galleons stand in early May like broad-fingered, upstretched hands, their crowns still leafless. A broken branch of willow, which drifted down the gull in the 1930s, now stands 60 feet tall at the head of the lake below the front of the main house. It rises from a thicket of its own fallen limbs, which have re-rooted themselves in the deep alluvial sand that surrounds it. Nearby, two veteran sweet chestnut trees are emerging from several decades of strategic retreat, their stag-headed crowns now disappearing amid a seasonal surge of new branches. They must have been prominent in the landscape known by George Crabbe when he lived at Great Glemham Hall. The house has gone, but the chestnuts look likely to last another 200 years.

In the kitchen garden, some of the old fruit trees, though shorter lived, are becoming veterans in their own right. Many have lost their insides to rot. Like the oaks in the park and at White House Farm, they have survived on hollowed-out stems. Others, like Annie Elizabeth, which were shunted sideways by the sheer force of the hurricane in

1987, have spent subsequent decades slowly re-aligning themselves. A few – such as Lord Derby and Lord Suffield – stagger on with the help of metal props and supports. Lord Suffield, which stands by Charlie Chandler's old shed (the one with the ominous well inside), is enjoying a remarkable second wind after losing almost all of its trunk. Lord Derby, with an espaliered span of almost 40 feet, has lost one of its long side limbs to decay, but the other side is still healthy. Annie Elizabeth, now growing at a curious angle, is, as Tessa observed, still able to put on a good show. But among these old trees, May can also be a sad month. As buds break and blossom erupts from their branches, it soon becomes apparent which trees have finally given up the ghost during the winter. The loss is eased by the presence of grafted replacements. Lord Derby, although on his last legs – or, in this case, one half of a heavily gnarled hollow trunk – has sported a number of progeny through the expert care of the plantsman Ivan Dickings. These are kept in pots by the fruit cage until they are ready to be planted out, often alongside the parent trees.

As with trees, so it is with people. The oldest members of the community become vessels of knowledge and local social history. Tom Eley, like Charlie Chandler, lived in Great Glemham village for almost all his life. His grandfather was a leading light in the Suffolk Land Workers' movement during the late 19th century. Tom managed the kitchen garden for seven years in the 1940s, while my father's family and that of my great uncle Antony Gathorne-Hardy all lived at White House Farm*. Tom followed in the footsteps of his own father, Horace Eley, who had worked as my grandfather's factor or caretaker at Great Glemham in the 1920s. He was born quite late in his father's life. Some of Tom's first-hand stories had their roots in the second half of the 19th century. I

* Antony was a ship's doctor in the Merchant Navy. His wife Ruth and their two sons joined my grandmother and her children at the farm. The children's names - Gay, Juliet, Sophie, Tina, Hugh, Jonny and Sam – were later used by Benjamin Britten for the characters in his opera *The Little Sweep*. More recently I came across a box of documents that included a six-page list of coded phrases drawn up by my great uncle Antony. These seem to have been created for letters and telegrams sent home to his wife Ruth while she was living at the farm in Great Glemham during the War. ";- I pulled six teeth out" indicated that he was in the West Mediterranean. ";- I'm so glad Jock has got the mains fixed on to the farm" was code for "We picked up survivors of an English bomber". A letter ending ";- Well, chin-chin" meant that the ship he was on had been bombed and was badly damaged.

remember him talking about the excavation of the lake in front of the
main house. I interrupted him to say that I could remember this as well.
(In the mid 1970s the lake was let to a local fishing club, which hired
plant to remove a deep sediment of silt and mud. Unbeknown to anyone,
the army had dumped training bombs and phosphorus bombs in the
water at the end of World War II. When the excavator broke them, the
sloppy mud hissed and bubbled, emitting steaming white flames.) Tom
shot me an annoyed look, asking how I could possibly remember what he
was about to relate. I explained that I had been there in the 1970s and
described a flaming shovel of mud as evidence. "Not then!" he replied. I
asked him which excavation was he talking about, for I knew of no other.
"Back in the 1890s – in my father's time," he answered.

To hear someone tell a tale that spanned 110 years, just one step
from the source, is an uncommon thing. Tom sadly died two years later,
but I remember his stories vividly, and their extraordinary reach.
He talked of fishing for pike in quiet pools along the Upper Alde;

of carpentry work for water mills; and of his father's initials, etched in a small glass pane on one of the old greenhouses in the garden. With his passing went many more stories, and another last bastion of a lexicon that was intimate to the land of Suffolk. Just as the veteran trees that punctuate the landscape around the garden at Great Glemham offer clues to past land use and settlement patterns, so too does the local language. Words that were once common are now as rare as the bittern or bee orchid: battlings, Betsy Janes, feetings, Civil Sues, mavises, Jacobites, spirkets and pikles – to name but a few. (See Appendix IV for some more.) Oral history knowledge and tradition that went back centuries have virtually disappeared overnight.

The spoken word, passed on from generation to generation, and shared within each, is a rich leavening for daily life. When Charlie Chandler died at home, Alan Sharpe (who had taken over the management of the garden from Charlie's successor David Coles) was dismayed to see many old jam jars of pickles and bottles of wine being placed in a skip. Knowing that they were "too old to use, but too precious to be thrown away", he dug a deep trench in one of the vegetable beds and emptied the contents into the ground. The following year, sweetcorn planted over this buried treasure grew exceptionally tall and bore huge, fat cobs. Alan nicknamed it "Charlie's sweetcorn". Perhaps, in doing so, he gave a name to an important reality of life in the garden: its productivity at any one time is partly due to the effort of that year; but it is also a legacy of the labour and knowledge of all those whose went before.

By the end of May, the production in the garden is gathering momentum. Like the old boilers that once warmed the greenhouses, it is building up a good head of steam. More and more vegetables and fruits are coming on line. Peas, beans and gooseberries are beginning to swell. Lettuces are ready and asparagus is in season, its long tender shoots pushing up through a thick layer of chicken manure and wood ash. In the hedgerows along nearby lanes, wild garlic, hop shoots and the first elderflowers are all ready to pick, together with other more spicy or scented wild plants such as Jack-by-the-Hedge and, in the Alde, Water Mint. From May onwards the increasing activity in the gardens is echoed in the kitchen with the cooking of more fresh ingredients, preparation of syrups and the arrival of new season spring lamb from our flock of crossbred mule ewes at White House Farm.

Carrot Soup

Caroline Cranbrook

This recipe also works well with peas, beetroot or cauliflower.

450g cooked carrots
1 small chopped onion
30g butter
2 tablespoons of flour
About 300ml water reserved from boiling the carrots
200ml milk
200-300ml stock
1 handful of finely chopped parsley
Ground black pepper & salt
Grated nutmeg

Sweat the onion in butter until tender and transparent. Mix in the chopped cooked carrots. Stir in flour and continue stirring for a few moments until it is incorporated. Gradually add the carrot water, milk and stock, stirring continuously. Season to taste adding a little nutmeg. Simmer for about ten minutes and finish by dropping in the finely chopped parsley. Blend. Sometimes I also add a tablespoonful of fresh orange juice or a little sugar if the carrots have been in store. I use this method for a variety of other vegetables, sometimes adding finely chopped potato with the onions, and varying the herbs and seasoning according to the vegetable.

Roast Alde Valley Lamb™

Jason Gathorne-Hardy

Poline Bala from Bario in the Kelabit Highlands of Sarawak taught me this recipe.

1 leg (or shoulder) of new season lamb
4 tablespoons of olive oil
1 to 1½ teaspoons of sea salt
4 large cloves of fresh garlic
1 tablespoon of local runny honey
3 tops/sprigs of fresh rosemary
5 tablespoons of Sarawak pepper

Place the leg of lamb in a lightly oiled baking tray. Cut narrow slots in the meat – each about an inch deep. Cut the cloves of garlic into angled thirds and push a wedge into each slot. Rub in olive oil over the whole joint. Rub the sea salt over the top side of the joint and then sprinkle a thick covering of pepper on top. Dribble the honey over this. Cut the rosemary into one and a half inch lengths and push one piece into each of the slots. Pour a tablespoon of oil on to the bottom of the tray around the joint. Place in an oven pre-heated to 220C. Leave for 20 minutes and then turn the heat down to 180C. After 1¼ hours, check the joint with a skewer. It is done when the juice from inside the joint runs clear. Use the oil and juice in the tray to make your gravy.

Rhubarb & Elderflower Custard

Claire Bruce-Clayton

This rich, eggy custard is perfumed with elderflower combined with tart, gloriously coloured rhubard stems.

For the Flowers and Rhubarb
600ml double cream
1 good handful of elderflowers
600-700g rhubarb
2 heaped tablespoons of sugar
1 orange
1 split vanilla pod
30g of root ginger
1 cupful of water

For the Custard
6 egg yolks
1 teaspoon of cornflour
125g of caster sugar

Pour 600ml of double cream into a saucepan. Add a good handful of well-rinsed elderflowers. Allow the blossoms to infuse in the cream for 30 minutes or so before straining through a sieve. Meanwhile poach the rhubarb. Cut the stalks into even-sized pieces and put them in a baking tray with two tablespoons of sugar, the orange cut into slices, the split vanilla pod and the chunk of root ginger. Add a cupful of water, cover and place in a medium oven for about 20 minutes or until the fruit is tender.

For the custard, beat together the 6 egg yolks, the teaspoon of cornflour and 125g caster sugar until thick and pale. Pour the still warm, strained elderflower cream over the beaten egg mixture, stir together and return to the pan. Stir the custard continuously over a low heat until it thickens, making sure it does not get too hot. Allow the rhubarb and custard to cool to room temperature before serving, otherwise you run the risk of the tart fruit curdling the custard.

As a variation, chill the custard and fruit, add some whipped cream and stir loosely together for an early summer fool, to eat with crisp almond biscuits. Or, if you have the time, make a rhubarb, elderflower and almond trifle by draining the rhubarb and mixing the juice with a softened leaf gelatine. Put some hard amaretti biscuits into a glass dish, pour over the rhubarb jelly and allow to set. Top this with the drained rhubarb, the cooled elderflower custard, the whipped cream and toasted almonds. A real treat!

June

Hot spell.
In the midday sun determined shadows
stay with the garlic plants.

The coal tits are busy ferrying their
food. Their nest is where the roof of
the salad house meets the wall.

Things are growing. I can hear them.
Bees, chives, sheep.

Tessa Newcomb

This page: Caring

June

Garden Notes

Sow radishes, beetroot, leeks, carrots, spring onions, onions. Hoe between young dwarf beans, onions, lettuce, sweetcorn, artichokes and asparagus. Tie up raspberries. Clear under gooseberries, currants, apples in the fruit cage. Tie up onions, peppers. Plant out kale, cabbage, sprouts, broccoli, spinach. Plant out chillies, peppers, aubergines, tomatoes and sweetcorn. Water greenhouses. Pick broad beans. Get blackbirds and thrushes out of fruit cage. Mark out and prepare squash beds. Plant out squashes. Clear peach house. Trim edges of grass paths. Remove cleavers from borders. Prepare lettuces for pubs and Lawsons Deli. Tie up roses. Clear lettuce bed and prepare new bed. Clear pond weed. Prick out cabbages. Trim vines and peaches. Dig up garlic. Harvest peas and broad beans.

SUNDAY IS GENERALLY not a good day to travel by train in East Anglia. Journeys between Suffolk and London tend to be a makeshift patchwork of bus rides and train hops as the lines are repaired and upgraded, even in the long summer months. But there is a stretch of track on the main line between Manningtree and Ipswich along which the larger trains always seem to get up to full speed, regardless of delays on either side. When returning from trips away from the county I like to open a window at this point on the journey to breathe in the sweet Suffolk air and to watch the countryside whizz by. It is like a pastoral version of Bruce Forsyth's famous conveyor belt of goodies on his television programme *The Generation Game.* Marsh, pasture, embankment, brambles, barley field, wheat field, estuary, boat, green lane, road bridge, footpath and woodland. All rush by, blurred in the foreground, clear in the distance as the driver makes up for lost time.

This is just how June can feel in the kitchen garden. Everything is beginning to gather pace. The rush of summer has arrived. Sowing, harvesting, watering, pruning, dead-heading, thinning, hoeing, mowing, hand-weeding, re-seeding and transplanting all collide. Salad leaves, chard and spinach are at their lushest. Artichokes are ripening. New potatoes are ready. Fresh tender carrots are on the way. In the fruit cage, raspberries, red currants, white currants and the first gooseberries are all ripe, with blackcurrants following on. If March and April were excessively wet, cold or dry, June also becomes the month to catch up and make good the flower beds and vegetable patches.

Amid the gathering abundance of the summer months, there is also something much more subtle to enjoy: the scent of roses. More than 200 varieties are dotted around the house, kitchen garden and shrubberies. Some are common, but many are unusual or rare. Several were rescued by my mother from abandoned cottage gardens in East Suffolk in the 1970s, and one rampant musk rose came from Beckford's ruined chapel in Montserrat in Portugal. (My maternal grandparents were stationed there briefly in 1942, both working for MI6. A picture of the chapel by Suffolk painter Tim Fargher hangs in the dining room of our family home.) Another beautiful specimen is the pink "Doddington Rose", trained up a whitewashed wall in the peach house. It was taken as a cutting from my mother's childhood home in Lincolnshire. The warmth of the greenhouse brings it into flower early. Its large heads start to fill out at the end of March, with repeats in June and later in the year. Its scent is quite phenomenal: sticking one's nose into it is like diving into a lagoon of fragrance, the surface a layer of thick petals, soft as satin. Along with gallica and rugosa varieties, its flowers are excellent for making syrups and tinctures.

Outside the peach house, the main herbaceous borders in the walled garden are backed by lines of rugosas, gallicas and hybrid musks. The gallicas have a milder scent but their petals are richly pigmented – an ice cream mixture of crimsons, deep purple and sometimes even blotched or striped. The rugosas produce very large

hips in late summer. They are big enough to be treated as a real fruit and are excellent for making syrup – in the 1940s, my mother remembers the government sponsoring the picking of wild rose hips to be put to this same use. Another beautifully scented rose is a variegated gallica called Rosa Mundi, or Fair Rosamond's Rose. It is said to have been named after Henry II's mistress, Fair Rosamund Clifford, with whom he started an affair in 1173. Next to the main house, a yellow *Rosa banksiae* grows up an east-facing wall and into the stable yard, spreading over at least 48 square yards of cream-coloured Woolpit brickwork. Its bundles of small custard yellow flowers are wonderful as a decoration – I use them as a table dressing in the barns at White House Farm during the Alde Valley Spring Festival. Further down the east front of the house, Etoile d'Hollande, another early-flowering variety, mounts a healthy challenge to the *Rosa banksiae* around the dining room windows with a profusion of heavily scented dark red flowers. At its feet, four or five varieties of Portland Rose form a thicket – their flowers also perfect for culinary use.

To the west of the house, beyond two lawns and a pair of mature Irish yews, a Rambling Rector lives up to its name, throwing out cascades of white blossom over the sparse canopies of some beleaguered apple trees beneath it. The scene reminds me of one of Maggi Hambling's sea paintings: a tumbling froth of blossom breaking over the green trees and lawn beneath. A few yards away, a collection of large limestone blocks salvaged from the old Snape bridge stand in piles around a quince tree. As toddlers, my brother, sister and I spent many hours crawling among the stones, hiding in the yarrow and grass-fringed cavities beneath them. The Rambling Rector also brings to mind the words of The Reverend George Crabbe's son, in his biography of his father.

> *"The summer evenings especially, at this place, dwell on my memory like a delightful dream. When we had finished our lessons, if we did not adjourn with my father to the garden to work in our own plats, we generally took a family walk through the green lanes around Glemham; where, at every turn, stands a cottage or farm, and not collected into a street, as in some parts of the kingdom, leaving the land naked and forlorn. Along these we wandered sometimes till the moon had risen, – my mother leading a favourite little niece who lived with us, my father reading some novel aloud, while my brother and I caught moths or other insects to add to his collection."*

There is a resonance here that links the centuries. From research organised by the writer Graham Fawcett, it is clear that Crabbe's interest in his surroundings extended beyond a sometimes brutally anti-romantic honesty about rural life to a passionate pursuit of natural history and, in particular, botany. Plants that were rare in his day are now forgotten and weeds that were so common to be unworthy of mention in the 18th century are now sufficiently rare to be called endangered. The roll call of plants that we have lost is long, but given George Crabbe's interest in natural history, garden plats and evening walks in the beautiful local landscape, it seems fitting that the Rambling Rector stands atop the hill his son described "enthroned in whitethorn and oak" – an inadvertent memorial to Suffolk's flinty poet.

Pea Soup

Caroline Cranbrook

June is the time when vegetable production in the garden goes into overdrive. This soup is a nice way of using up peas.

570gm fresh peas
1 lettuce heart
110gm of butter
¾l of water
2 teaspoons of sugar
Salt
Fresh spearmint

Melt the butter. Add the shredded lettuce, peas, salt and sugar. Cover and stew gently for about 10 minutes. Add the water and cook until the peas are tender. Liquidise. Add seasoning. Serve either hot or cold with finely chopped fresh mint in a side dish, to scatter over the peas.

Beef Carpaccio with Salad Leaves

Lola de Mille

Named after the rich red and whites used by the Renaissance painter Vittore Carpaccio, beef carpaccio is a dish of very thinly sliced raw meat, traditionally served drizzled with a mustard mayonnaise. In this version, the beef is rolled in herbs and seared, then dressed with olive oil and a tangy balsamic vinegar. The simplicity and clean flavours are perfect for showing off a few choice ingredients, such as the first tender leaves from the summer salad patch.

500g of centre-cut organic/free range fillet of beef
Dijon mustard
Rosemary, thyme, cracked black peppercorns
Maldon sea salt
Olive oil
Radicchio or young salad leaves, such as rocket, red mustard or baby chard
Pecorino or parmesan cheese
Fig balsamic vinegar
Pine nuts or capers – whichever you prefer

Ask for the beef to be cut as one piece, with the fat and sinews trimmed off. With a pastry brush, coat the outside with a thin layer of Dijon mustard. Sprinkle the chopped herbs and seasoning on a

board and roll the fillet over them so
that it is covered evenly. Add a little
olive oil to a very hot heavy-
bottomed frying pan or flat griddle,
sear the beef on both sides, leaving
it about a minute between turning.
Remove and cool. Wrap it tightly in
grease-proof paper or cling-film
and place in the freezer for an hour.
In the meantime wash and spin-dry
the salad leaves. Remove the beef
from the freezer and unwrap.
Finely slice the beef, using the full
length of the blade of a long, sharp
knife. Arrange the slices of beef,
slightly overlapping, on a large
platter. Season well. Shave the
cheese into thin strips, using a
potato peeler, and scatter over the
salad leaves. Drizzle with a good
fruity olive oil and the balsamic
vinegar. Pine nuts or capers are a
nice addition to this dish.

Broad Beans &
Breadcrumbs
Caroline Cranbrook/Mary Taylor Simeti

The broad bean is one of our most
ancient cultivated vegetables. It has
been found in Swiss Bronze Age
deposits and was cultivated by the
Greeks, Romans and Ancient
Egyptians, all of whom believed the
beans had magical properties of
various kinds. For instance, the
Greeks thought their hollow stalks
provided the spirits of the dead with
a direct route to Hades. The
following recipe is from Mary
Taylor Simeti's book *Sicilian Food –
Recipes from Italy's Abundant Isle*.

1.8kg fresh young beans
225ml water
225ml of olive oil
1 cup-full of stale white breadcrumbs
1 tablespoon of white wine vinegar
Fresh spearmint

The beans must be small and young.
Otherwise they have to be skinned,
which is a very laborious activity.
Cook in the water with the olive oil.
Cover and boil for 10 minutes or so,
until the beans are tender. Add
finely chopped mint, breadcrumbs,
vinegar, oil, ground black pepper
and salt to taste. (Summer or winter
savory can be substituted for the
mint for an extra layer of slightly
smoky flavour.)

July

New French bean plants. Tender
green tendrils on the sturdy wigwam –
dark against the strong light.

A team of peppers lined up
in a box. "Worldbeaters" in a
box labelled "Holland".

The growth of everything is no
longer contained. Becomes
worrying. Chris tries to hoe.

A green shield bug lands on the sundial.

Tessa Newcomb

This page: Garlic

July

Garden Notes

Finish harvesting peas and broad beans. Pick gooseberries. Tie in peppers and aubergines. Pot on young grafted fruit trees. Feed chrysanthemums. Plant remaining sweetcorn. Weed and hoe vegetable beds. Tie in tomatoes. Lift shallots. Rotavate new area for leeks. Water vines, peach, nectarine and apricot. Pick courgettes and summer savory. Lift onions to dry. Lift and start bagging potatoes for storage. Plant leeks. Spray cabbages against cabbage white caterpillars. Start harvesting peaches and nectarines. Flood chilli house to water all plants. Hoe vegetable beds. Harvest apricots.

IN HIS CONTRIBUTION to *A Tribute to Benjamin Britten on His Fiftieth Birthday* my grandfather noted that the original Bill for the Ipswich, Norwich and Yarmouth Railway presented a route that followed the River Alde past Great Glemham through the villages of Sweffling and Rendham. Local opposition in the mid 19th century led to the line being moved further east. The modern Lowestoft Line, heavily pruned of smaller side branches to Framlingham and Aldeburgh by Beeching's cuts in the 1960s, runs through Westerfield, Woodbridge, Melton, Campsea Ashe, Saxmundham, Darsham, Halesworth and Beccles. Sweffling and Rendham survive as quiet, relatively secluded villages tucked into the heavily wooded landscape of the Upper Alde Valley. There is a gentle rivalry between the two settlements. I was once told that this was because the villages were on different sides in the English Civil War, but the story-teller could not remember which village was on which side. "Glemham", by some accounts, means "the village of Glem" or "Glen". Another theory is that "Glemham" means "happy village".

As far as I know, Great Glemham did not align itself with either side in the Civil War, perhaps maintaining a position of contented independence. But almost three hundred years later, conflict left very profound marks upon the parish. The Great War of 1914-1918 took many young men. Their names are listed on the village war memorial. Fourteen men from a village of only two hundred and fifty people, including five from two families: George Johnson, Lewis Johnson, Stanley Mattin, Frederick Mattin and John Mattin – alongside Ernest Pleasance, Ernest Stone, Frederick Pendle, Arthur Close-Brooks and others. Twenty five years later, the Second World War brought further casualties and rationing, the Women's Land Army and the requisitioning of both Glemham House and a large area of farm land on high ground between the villages of Great Glemham, Parham and Marlesford. This was cleared to make a military airfield – one of more than 40 which were built in East Anglia. I once spoke to Herman Kindred, a much respected local farmer from Parham, about this process.

He described the pre-War landscape as being dominated by a patchwork of small fields and hedges. There were more than 40 fields all together, with a small area of wet unimproved land on the southern side. Charlie Chandler described this as "Marlesford Common" and said it was used each spring and summer by Romany families as a seasonal campsite.

To create the airfield – an elongated "A" arrangement of three main runways surrounded by a perimeter track, plane turn-around pads and bomb dumps - almost 400 acres of farm land had to be cleared and flattened. Paul Berry, a fourth generation timber man from Framlingham, passed on several stories from his father, the local timber merchant Jim Berry. One described how dynamite was used to clear oak trees from the land. Bundles of explosives were packed beneath their roots and then detonated with a fuse cord. Whole trees were blasted out of the ground. When viewed from afar, a soggy boom would arrive after the timber was airborne, amid showers of hedgerow and heavy clay.

Glemham House, located about half a mile north of what became known as Parham or Framlingham airfield, was first made available to evacuee children and was then requisitioned by the army. With at least 4,000 ground support staff and air crew living at Parham Airfield and the main house full of soldiers, the population of Great Glemham and Parham must have soared. The house was shot at once by a roving enemy fighter plane (there are apparently bullet holes in the rafters, though I have never seen them) and a B17 Flying Fortress belonging to the 890th Bomb Group at Parham crashed through a wall that surrounds the park. It had been shot down by an enemy fighter plane. It was about to cartwheel into a field called New Road south of the park when one of its wings clipped an elm tree in the hedge line. This flipped the plane into a more level approach. A few hundred yards further on it belly-flopped through the park wall. Once again, providence intervened: as the plane crashed through the wall, its remaining bombs were stripped from the upper fusilage, which slid on through the ruined wall into the park. Seven of the ten crew survived, pulled from the wreckage by brave villagers. My grandfather salvaged a buckled propeller blade, twisted into a smooth wave-like curl at one end and pock-marked by a bullet. For many years it stood at the junction of two paths in the shrubberies as an informal war memorial. In the 1990s it was moved to a new site and formally dedicated to the crew of the plane, both casualties and survivors, and to the 890th Bomb Group. Surviving members of the crew flew from the United States for a ceremony of dedication, burying a small time capsule in the propeller's new brick and concrete plinth.

The interior of the house bears more subtle marks of military use. In the cellar, heavily worn steps lead down to a long passage. On one of the walls a plan drawn in pencil outlines various storage rooms: "Kit Bags", "Ammunition" and "Sten Guns". As a boy I found this last inscription impossibly tantalising, leading to all sorts of fantasies about abandoned munitions and weapons. Exploration of dark corners and a disused coal store led nowhere. Even the most promising room revealed nothing – a tiny air chamber built around a subterranean stove for underfloor heating. It was only after the lake was excavated that real explosives turned up, in the form of phosphorus bombs. Playing on the bank of the lake the following summer, I found a rounded piece of metal with a deeply satisfying yellow ring around its tip sticking out of the ground. I spent several hours playing Bomb Disposal with my penknife, slowly unearthing the nose cone of a two foot long mortar bomb. Fantastically pleased with the results of my careful excavation, I ran back to the house to fetch my father, who, I think, turned a snowy shade of white and called the police. A real Bomb Disposal team turned up and inspected it. Fortunately it was a practice bomb, its heavy head filled with sand. Both the bomb and I survived: it now lies propped up against a wall at my farm, and I am writing these words!

Another more curious incident was a surprise visit in the early 1980s by a war-time resident of the house. My brother and I happened to be at home alone one day when the front door bell rang. Upon opening it we were presented with a tall man and a smart-looking black car. He introduced himself as Frank Cooper "the Marmalade Man". He explained that he had been stationed in the main house in the early 1940s. We remembered severe warnings about not talking to strangers, and certainly not letting them indoors, but judged that a tall man who called himself the "Marmalade Man" was certainly interesting, and probably genuine. It seemed a very unlikely cover for a burglar. I think in the back of our minds we also hoped that he might be able to reveal the whereabouts of the elusive stash of forgotten sten guns that I was sure still lay hidden somewhere in the cellar.

We showed him the neatly inscribed lists of soldiers' names on wooden shutters in the bedrooms and the map on the walls in the cellar, but to no avail. No guns and no marmalade. I am not sure if we ever told our parents about the encounter. I had, I think, previously blown the top off a thermometer by placing its bulb against an electric blower heater in an attempt to show my mother that I had a temperature – which always justified a day off school. With the fire still on, bits of glass all around me and the stump of the thermometer in my hand, the evidence against me

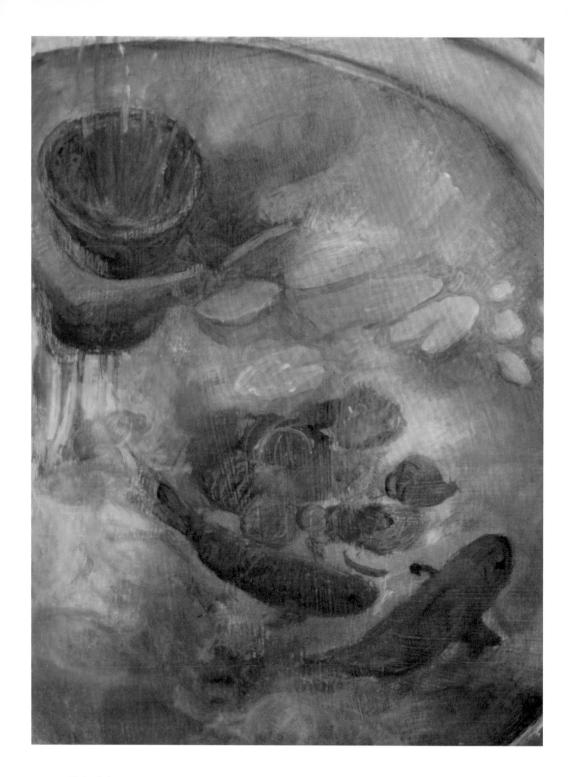

was overwhelming. I remember racking through my mental filing system of excuses, but could find nothing that would be remotely credible. After this experience, I had an inner awareness of which stories were honest and reasonably realistic, and which sounded plain daft: letting a stranger called the "Marmalade Man" into the house to look at war graffiti and maps in the cellar while our parents were out rated very low on the credibility scale, and there is nothing more frustrating for a child than to be disbelieved when telling the truth.

During the early 1940s, as marine supply convoys were struggling to cross the Atlantic (with my great uncle Antony possibly writing "I simply must write to Aunt Jane – there is an epidemic of stinking throats and flu on board" meaning "We are in Scapa Flow and have boarded a neutral ship"), Britain became more and more isolated. Among the many public information campaigns, one battle cry still resonates today, but thankfully for very different reasons: "Dig for Victory". Today, one of the challenges facing communities is not warfare between nations, but the need to feed ourselves more sustainably: to cut out waste, to reduce energy requirements and to re-localise both the production and distribution of foods. On the ground – and by this I mean within individual families and broader communities – there seems to be a resurgent urge and desire to garden and grow food – and, possibly, for farms to become more like gardens. Knowledge is crucial to this process, but a more fundamental requirement is access to land and good soil: well-manured, free-draining, well-aerated soil with a balanced supply of micro-nutrients and a vibrant micro-flora is the bedrock of healthy gardening – on any scale.

Given its exposed position and heavy clay subsoil, it is at first surprising that the kitchen garden at Glemham House is so productive. I remember talking to a friend and local organic farmer, Robert White from Peak Hill Farm in Theberton. He described how it had taken ten to fifteen years of digging muck into the heavy clay ground on his family's land before the nutrient content was consistently high enough to grow good crops of vegetables. His fields now produce some of the finest organic salad leaves in the county. The same rule has proved true for the kitchen garden at Great Glemham. The secret of its productivity is the huge amount of muck that is dug into the soil each year. But this richness does not come quickly, nor easily. Hundreds, possibly thousands, of tons of manure, night soil, leaf mould and compost have been incorporated into these two acres over the past 180 years.

Getting *underneath* gardening in this way is a fundamental aspect of good soil management. Deep digging or trenching helps aerate the earth and puts nutrients deep underground. It also supports a healthy micro-flora of useful fungi and bacteria, without which the soil would lose its vitality. Plain farmyard muck is a good start to restoring or improving soil structure and fertility, provided it has broken down before being applied, but it doesn't always deliver all the micro-nutrients and minerals that vegetables need to truly flourish. The experience with Charlie's legacy of giant sweetcorn revealed that there was something quite potent in old pickles and wines. Other more ordinary supplements can help, including wood ash (from woodburners and bonfires) and the residue from compost heaps or worm boxes.

The most demanding plants in the garden, in terms of nutritional support and general care, are probably the old grapes in the vine house. One legend attached to them is that the body of an old horse was interred in the feeder beds in front of the greenhouse in the 1820s to provide long-term nutrients for the vines. I have heard this story elsewhere, but do not know if it is true at Great Glemham. But today this bed in front of the vine house is used as a burial ground for small animals found dead in the garden and fields. Certainly, the grape vines require a much greater level of feeding and pruning than many other plants in the garden. Those at Glemham are lowered from their wire supports in December, pruned, brushed and peeled; re-hung in March; pruned again and then kept well-ventilated as the new shoots and grapes develop. The bunches of grapes are thinned several times in July and August as the fruit swell, until they are ready for picking in September and October. The walls are white-washed with lime and the earth around the vines' roots is kept clean – they stand in a deep brick-lined bed set inside the greenhouse.

In the late 1990s my sister Flora (who runs her own landscape and garden design company called Topio) helped plan the peach house as an outdoor teaching room, the intention being to use it as a space for shared learning about foods and gardening. With visits from local primary schools and adult training groups from the charity East Feast, this aim is slowly being fulfilled, for another challenge of modern life is to re-introduce students, especially younger children, to the tastes of "real food". Flavour enhancers, bulking agents, salt and sugar are now so prevalent in everyday processed foods that ordinary ingredients such as fruits, home-grown vegetables and less-processed meats or dairy products can often taste bland or even odd.

This was my experience one July when I was invited to present a small Alde Valley Food Adventure for students at a summer school held at a high school in Ipswich. The consensus was that a selection of plain yoghurt, flower syrups and cheeses all tasted boring, odd or even slightly unpleasant. Curiously, it was smoked mackerel from Pinney's Smokehouse in nearby Orford that proved decisive. It was almost universally liked and provoked a renewed interest in other foods that were available to taste. After that, russet apple juice (from High House Fruit Farm in Sudbourne) and a selection of fresh seasonal produce from the kitchen garden proved very popular. By the end of the session, general opinion had shifted to a position that local foods were interesting. The provision of information and choice was vital in this process. The students then chose ingredients to prepare a meal for their parents and families, which was presented on day two of the project. I hope knowledge-sharing and training days may become a larger part of the garden's work at Great Glemham, alongside its day-to-day existence as a source of fresh produce. This reaches a peak in July, after the first flush of young shoots and leaves in spring.

Gazpacho

Caroline Cranbrook

This iced vegetable soup epitomises the pleasures of summer food. It was probably introduced into Europe from the Middle East via Sicily. Today it is found throughout Spain and the Mediterranean. In Malaga it is made with almonds and grapes and in Extramadura with eggs and bread. It can be thick as porridge or thin as a consommé. The following recipe is based on the Andalusian version.

675g skinned tomatoes
1 green pepper
1 medium-sized onion
1 medium cucumber
2 cloves chopped garlic
2 tbs wine vinegar
¼ tsp sugar
2 tbs olive oil
1 cup water
Salt and pepper to taste
*Small squares of bread or croutons and
    diced vegetables as garnish*

Remove seeds and pith from the pepper and liquidise it with a little water. Add the remaining water, vinegar, oil and the rest of the ingredients. Liquidise again. Chill. Serve with separate side dishes of croutons or small pieces of bread, finely chopped onions, red pepper and tomato. The soup freezes well.

Roast Middle White Pork Shoulder

Miranda and William Kendall

Having converted our family farm to organic production we decided to go one stage further by producing a large range of produce under our brand, Maple Farm Kelsale. We have re-created a traditional mixed farm, also keeping rare breed Middle White pigs. These feed off the waste from the farm's Austrian stone-built flour mill and any vegetables that can't be sold. The Middle White was one of the many victims of post-war specialisation. It was bred by the Victorians to make the perfect pork chop. The quality of its meat is legendary – the Emperor of Japan has built a shrine in its honour in Tokyo. We use most of their meat for bacon, sausages and hams. Eating Middle White shoulder, slow-cooked, makes it hard to return to more mundane pork ever again.

Shoulder of Middle White pork
Several glasses of apple juice or cider
Fresh sage
Salt
Pepper

Season the joint with salt and pepper and put in a casserole or deep oven tray. Pour over a few glasses of apple juice or cider and

French Beans & Tomatoes

Caroline Cranbrook

add a handful of chopped sage. Put the lid on the casserole or cover the tray with a good layer of foil. Place in the slowest oven you can (ideally the plate warmer of an Aga) – little more than 40 C. Time in the oven will depend on the size of the joint but ideally a joint about 2.7 -3.7kg should remain there overnight. Put in at 11 in the evening, it will be ready by 10.30am but will hold well until lunchtime. It is virtually impossible to overcook it as it is always sitting in the copious quantities of fat which make the Middle White famous. When it is ready, the joint will be almost submerged in delicious liquid lard and the meat itself will be leaner than the average supermarket joint from an "industrial" pig. Half an hour before serving, remove the meat from the fat, peel off the skin, scrape off any underlying fat and then, closely watching to avoid burning, grill it or put it in a very hot oven to produce perfect crackling. The joint itself will barely need carving as it will collapse into delicious pieces of richly flavoured meat. Perfect for a winter lunch or for a summer garden feast, when it can be served with new potatoes, a strong-flavoured salad and cucumber pickles.

I remember thinking that I had invented this recipe but then found it in several cookery books. In the garden we grow four varieties of dwarf beans for using fresh. They are Purple Queen, the slender Safari, the golden Brittle Beure and the very prolific Delinel. Our favourite tomatoes are the black Russian, such as Krim, the Amish Brandywine, Golden Sunrise and the small luscious ones, Sweet Million and Black Cherry. We freeze some of the tomato harvest whole and the rest we pulp, using the highly efficient Rigamonti Passa Pomodori (available from Seeds of Italy). The frozen tomato puree is a wonderful basis for easy soups later on in the year.

450g French beans
1 clove garlic
3-4 medium-sized tomatoes
1 tbs olive oil
1 tbs chopped basil

Put the beans in boiling salted water and cook until tender. Drain them. Skin the tomatoes and cook them gently in the olive oil with the garlic, basil and salt to taste. When they are cooked pour over the beans. Very good hot or cold.

August

*The level of the fishpond
has dropped because there
are cracks in the concrete.*

*Stingy hot. Gathorne said
he had never seen so many roses.*
Tessa Newcomb

This page: Climbing

August

Garden Notes

Bag potatoes. Hoe remaining cabbage, leek and chard beds. Plant out cucumbers. Water beans. Treat aubergines for aphids. Hoe onion beds. Spray vines with fungicide. Harvest apples, beans, tomatoes and courgettes. Remove tomatoes affected by blight. Sort, trim and box onions for storage. Start harvesting sunrise squashes and beans for pubs. Tie up chrysanthemums and fruiting tomato plants. Remove sick or infected aubergine leaves. Plant lettuce and basil in chilli house. Rake garden paths. Clear up fallen apples. Trim and thin grapes. Lift and hang first bean plants to dry. Pick and deliver lettuces to farm shop and pubs. Hoe leeks and other beds.

A FEW YEARS AGO I swapped some dead standing oak trees for a large butt of elm wood. It lay among nettles and brambles at a sawmill in Sudbourne. With the aid of an old tractor and a complex system of chains and pulleys slung from a steel gantry, the mill's owner, Dick Murphy, carefully manoeuvred the huge lump of timber on to the deck of his band saw. It was an extraordinary sight. The gearing of the pulley was such that one man could lift a piece of wood the size of a large elephant up off the ground with one hand. I watched cautiously as it hung legless in the air, twisting gently as Dick swung it round into the shed and then lowered it on to the railed deck of the mill. After trimming large lumps off its flanks, we slid it slowly back and forth through the buzzing white line of the band saw. Although the tree had lain in the yard for almost eight years, its heartwood was still wet. With each steady pass of the wobbling blade, another page of its history opened up in a series of broad eight foot by two foot planks. The vagaries of its past – its rate of growth, amputated limbs, dry years and wet – lay wide open to read in a swirling orange grain still bright with the last remnants of its sap, hoarded over the years.

To be good with timber seems to require the combined skills of a farmer, historian and butcher. The location, growth form and bark of a tree can tell you much about the quality of its wood long before you lay a blade on to its surface. A knowledge of local history can contribute an understanding of soils and the likelihood of a tree being diseased or "shook up" inside. (Shake is used in the timber trade to describe internal splitting in standing trees. The cracks, which can run radially or concentrically up the inside of a tree trunk, are usually invisible from the outside, but can reduce the quality of timber from veneer to firewood.) Once a tree is felled and on the ground, knowing where to make the first cuts and then how to process it into planks, posts and beams will have a significant effect on its final value. Just as a butcher knows where to stop a shoulder cut and start a fillet, or how much fatty meat to trim off a roasting joint, so a good timber dealer or saw mill owner will know where to separate the butt of a tree from its first round of branches, or how best to plank a lump of wood to show off its grain and avoid any twists and knots that are concealed within it.

This knowledge is vital within the timber world, but it is increasingly rare. I remember talking to Paul Berry about his family and his inherited knowledge of timber. He is a fourth generation timber man. His father, Jim, bought much of the pine and oak that blew down at Great Glemham in 1987. I remember him describing the arrival of chain saws in the 1930s and 1940s. Many of the tree fellers who worked with him would set aside these new noisy machines as they approached the final stages of felling in order to hear the tree "talk". The final creaks and small cracks around the butt would tell the feller which way it was going to fall and whether it might jump back or bounce against the hinge of wood left inside the stump to guide its descent. I have always carried with me a word of advice that Jim gave me: if you or a workmate are felling a tree and it begins to fall in your direction, run towards the tree, not away. This sounds counter-intuitive, but if you follow this piece of advice, you will only have to roll sideways at the last minute to avoid being squashed. Run away from a falling tree, and you will have the whole crown to dodge, which is nearly impossible. Hanging on to this

information is like keeping an old bent pound coin in the dusty bottom of a coat pocket: one day, impossible as it seems, it might prove useful. I have never used it, but for that reason alone it seems worth passing on.

Today, we often treat timber simply as "wood". This is like treating beef, mutton, pork and lamb as "meat", without bothering to look at the almost endless variation in provenance, conformation, flavour and joints that can be made from different varieties of livestock – let alone respecting the source of our food, the animals from which the meat is derived. With its roots and foundations in the mid-Regency period, the garden at Great Glemham dates from a period in which the industrial revolution was quickly gathering pace, but in which the internal combustion engine, plastics and other synthetic materials were still unimagined and unknown. Craft workers and tradesmen of this era still had to apply an extensive working knowledge of the natural materials around them. With regard to timber, this often involved putting different kinds of wood to very specific uses. English elm was used for making chair seats and large cross beams; hornbeam furze was used as a fuel for bread ovens; ash was made into tool handles and spokes of cart wheels; pine into doors and window frames; and oak

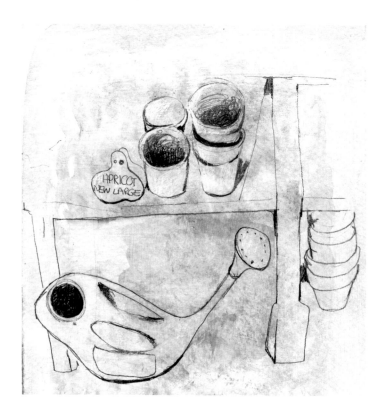

into almost everything else – floorboards, decking, panelling, beams, doors, soul plates and rafters.

Once, when walking past Tom Eley's house at the Timber Yard, I saw that the door to his workshop was open. I stopped to say hello. As we chatted, I noticed a small piece of wood lying in a dusty pile of unused – but possibly useful – offcuts at the end of a workbench. (Every cabinet maker or joiner's workshop seems to have a pile of these somewhere about the place – in a corner, under a workbench or stacked outside under cover.) The piece of wood was about the size of my hand, if held slightly cupped. It had ten facets and was cleanly cut. It was widest about its middle, which was rectangular in cross-section. From here, the wood tapered asymmetrically in both directions, terminating in differently sized square-cut ends. It was a very odd shape.

Seeing my curiosity, Tom first asked if I knew what wood it was made from. I said cherry, but it was apple. He then asked if I could guess what it was for. I didn't have a clue. I could not for the life of me see what it would fit into, nor how it could stay in place. He picked it up and, turning it over in his hands, explained that it was a tooth for a wooden drive wheel in a watermill; and that it would have been wedged into a tight-fitting socket lined with tarred hessian or some similar textile. He had kept it as a memento from a repair job he had worked on in the 1970s. It was an extraordinary object. I turned it over in my own hands, feeling its weight and its smooth, peculiar surfaces. It was like reading Braille. The odd angles, the asymmetric form and the surprising density of the wood all made sense. Each facet seemed to relate a different aspect of its history: the use of apple, instead of cherry, ash or oak; the wooden mechanics of a water mill; the power that came from running water; Tom's knowledge of timber and carpentry, partly learned from his father, Horace Eley; and the explanation of how the tooth had come to be lying quietly in Tom's workshop in Great Glemham. It was like a one-page book.

Walking up the Dell from the Timber Yard to the house, this small piece of apple wood seemed to me to symbolise some of the lost knowledge that lurks hidden in the garden, built into its structures. I looked again at the old tools, furniture and fittings. Who had made them? What wood had they used? And how had they applied it? In the potting shed, the metalwork of almost every tool is set into lengths of slender, straight-grained ash – supple and hard. Axe handles are oval in cross-section, with a kick at the end – all adding to the swing, balance and grip of the whole. The elongated handles of old cromes, pitchforks and rakes have a thin section before a fattened end, enabling them to be flicked out and then caught by a tightening of the grip. The hafts of bill-hooks and flashers are broad and fat in the hand, with a notch or snub-ended beak at the end, sometimes pierced by a hole for a wrist cord. The notch helps when chopping more remote branches. The workbench and the awkward chest of drawers are made from close-grained pine. The kitchen side chairs are made of beech and elm. Old floor boards in the bothy were cut from larch or Douglas fir, sometimes with the grain of alternating boards cupped in different directions. The original frames of the greenhouses – repaired by Tom's father, Horace Eley, in 1931 – were constructed from old growth pitch pine set on oak plinths.

The contrast in the quality of the original timbers used in the garden compared to those available today is at times striking. Most tool handles today are metal, plastic or made from rare but cheap tropical hardwoods. Where ash is used, it is often straight cut. Subtle design features which aided the grip or handling of a tool have often been lost. Timber used in construction is generally fast-grown pine from young plantations or clear-felled forest. It is common to find four or five growth rings per inch, compared to old-growth pine in the bothy and potting shed, which can have as many as 25 rings in the same span. Such slow-grown pine is so heavy with resin that it will last for decades, even when exposed to the elements. Without preservatives, structures made of soft young-growth pine will often only last a few years. Tools and materials are now much cheaper and more easily acquired, which is good. But, in global terms, huge areas of forest are consumed every year to supply products which may not last long. At the same time, at home in England, we use our woodlands perhaps less than we have ever done.

The end of August, in my mother's words, brings with it a "monumental late summer harvest". Beans, squashes, peppers, aubergines, plums, damsons, late courgettes and blackberries are all ripe and ready to be gathered in. Beans have become one of the most prominent crops of the walled garden under my parents' stewardship. Eighteen varieties are grown: six for eating fresh and twelve for drying. They include Borlotti Lingua di Fuoca and Trail of Tears, a first nation North American bean grown by the Cherokee Indians (surviving members of the tribe took the beans with them on the long forced march to Oklahoma under the Indian Removal Act of 1830). Another variety is a giant white butter bean from the southern Mediterranean, originally bought in Padua market. The most beautiful of all is a multi-coloured

Hungarian bean, originally bought from a market stall in Budapest. Red, purple, white and brown splashed with blotches of black, a handful are perfect for re-telling *Jack and the Beanstalk* to younger cousins and nephews. All the varieties, once shelled, have the feel of an early currency … or perhaps a future one. Weight for weight, a small handful of beans can certainly prove themselves more useful than the equivalent weight of alloy coins or gold.

In contrast to the delicate nature of bean pods and their vines, the squashes that lurk under their own foliage in the garden look like exotic livestock. Their names live up to their shapes: The Gourd of Naples; Tromba d'Albenga (or Tromboncino); Serpente di Sicilia. Of these, the Gourd of Napoli is the largest. They begin to emerge from their foliage in August, their dark green forms looking like the backs of small pigs foraging in the vegetable patch. My mother first grew the Serpente di Sicilia as a mystery vegetable, training it up the side of the semi-derelict peach house. Within two months, the plants had sprawled up and over almost the entire greenhouse. Tendrilled stems were even clambering over the top of the garden wall, twelve feet above the ground. The sheer weight of the plants, with their long fruit hanging like truncated snakes from the greenhouse roof, led to the partial collapse of the building – and its subsequent restoration. Once in the late 1990s, quite how or why I can't remember, I was waiting for a Circle Line train at Monument station in London with a backpack and a very large Serpente di Sicilia. A family from Bangladesh came up to ask me where the vegetable was from. I explained that it had been grown in Suffolk. When they asked what we called them, I said that I didn't know. They said their name for them was "dodi". I asked them how they cooked them, since this had also been a mystery. Their answer was that they were best eaten when still small – certainly not when they were as long as an outstretched arm or leg. They have since become one of the garden's signature vegetables, alongside the chillies, beans and, more recently, a growing stable of huge conical cabbages (Filderkraut and its red-coloured relative Kalibos) from Germany.

Courgettes & Summer Savory

Caroline Cranbrook

We grow several varieties of courgettes including the dark green Nero di Milano, the white Lungo Bianco, the yellow Goldrush, the ridged Romanesco and the round Tondo di Piacenza.

Courgettes
Garlic
Chopped herbs (eg parsley, basil, summer or winter savory, or marjoram)
Salt
Pepper

Top, tail and slice the courgettes (crossways or lengthways). I usually cook them slowly in olive oil with garlic and herbs. They can be eaten hot or cold or pureed in a blender which, with the addition of chicken stock, make a nice soup. It is a good way of using up a glut and freezes well. Alternatively, the courgettes can be dipped in a light batter made from iced water (or lager) with flour (or chickpea flour) added gradually, beaten with a fork to the consistency of cream and the slices then quickly fried in hot olive oil. The same method works well for sliced aubergines.

Chicken with Vegetables

Sukie Hemming

1 good free-range chicken
6 well-flavoured good-sized tomatoes or 20 small plum tomatoes
Pitted black olives (in quantity about 1/3 of the tomatoes when chopped)
Chopped garlic cloves
A chopped bunch of flat-leaved parsley
A few sprigs of thyme
1 lemon
Extra virgin olive oil

Rub the outside of the chicken with a small amount of olive oil and place in a ceramic or metal roasting dish. Chop the tomatoes and mix with the olives, garlic, parsley and thyme leaves. Grate the zest from the lemon into the mix and add the juice from half of the lemon. Season with coarse salt and roughly ground black pepper. Pour in enough olive oil to ensure that the mix is well-coated and stir briefly. Spoon the mixture into the chicken cavity until it is full and then place the rest around the chicken in the dish. Put the second half of the lemon at the end of the chicken cavity to keep the mixture inside during cooking and infuse the stuffing with the lemon juice. Roast at about 200C to start with and then a lower heat of 180C. To serve, scoop out contents of the chicken into the dish.

Chard, Blue Cheese & Walnuts

Marcia Blakenham & Stephanie Bullard

Chard is available most of the year, is easy to grow, and comes in a variety of colours with beautifully crinkled leaves. Ruby chard is especially striking.

230g short-crust pastry
350g chard
175g blue cheese (not too strong)
3 eggs
A small pot of cream
A small handful of walnuts
A pinch of ground nutmeg
Seasoning

Blind bake the pastry in a flan dish. Cook the chard in a little water with a pinch of nutmeg and strain well. Beat together eggs and cream, adding chard, walnuts and cheese cut or crumbled into small nuggets. Pour into a prepared flan and sprinkle with a little more nutmeg. Bake at 180C for 25 minutes.

Squidgle-Squadgle Apricots

Fidelity Cranbrook/Gathorne Cranbrook

Ripe apricots can be a little dull when compared with the peaches and nectarines that follow them in the greenhouse. But they make the most delicious jam, far juicier than the bland, sweet and sticky orange-coloured paste that appears sometimes on supermarket shelves. They also make a very delicious version of my late mother's best-loved pudding, which her grandchildren all knew as "squidgle-squadgle".

Fresh apricots (or tinned)
Bananas
Sugar
Double cream

Halve the apricots and remove the stones. Half-fill a pan with the apricots and add a little water to prevent the fruit from sticking to the bottom. Stew fairly rapidly, stirring with a wooden spoon. Add sugar to taste. Allow to cool. Peel and slice some bananas (about 1/3 the volume of the apricots) and with about the same amount of double cream, add to the apricots. Liquidise and place in the fridge for a couple of hours before serving.

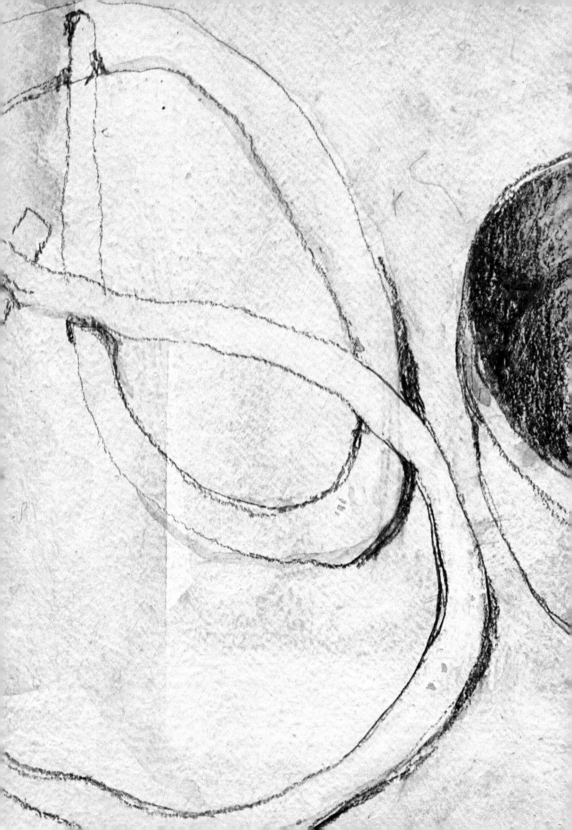

September

*Between the box hedges a carpet
of weeds curve up behind the rake.*

*This terrible decay.
The pole stands alone.
The single tomato's pink flesh
rots slowly home. Their plants
scarred by blight.*

Tessa Newcomb

This page: The empty pot

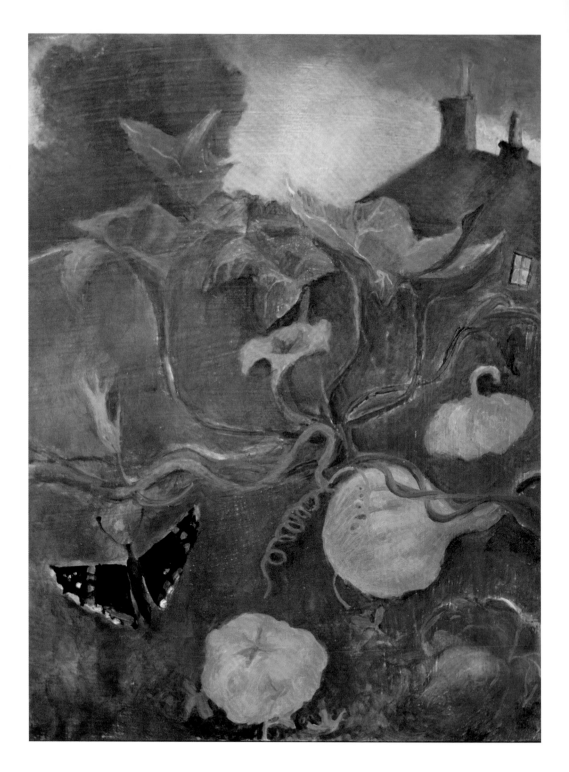

September

Garden Notes

Harvest tomatoes, cucumbers, aubergines, courgettes, peppers, chillies and squashes – nearly the last of the season. Trim blight on tomatoes. Fork over sweet peas. Pick damsons and plums. Lift Croatian dwarf beans. Put onions, garlic and shallots in apple store for the winter. Hoe around runner beans and squashes. Remove mildew-infected leaves from courgettes. Plant out wallflowers. Water vines. Lift "chilli con carne" beans and hang in barrow shed to dry. Clear dead leaves from peach house. Hoe under box hedges along garden paths. Stake peppers. Clean all greenhouses of dead leaves. Move potted chrysanthemums into greenhouse. Throw out rotten apples, onions and shallots from the store. Move chicken runs. Harvest sweet pears and figs.

STANDING BY THE dipping pond in the middle of the walled garden gives a clear view of its four entrances. To the south-east is a large pine door, about seven and a half feet tall by four feet wide, set beneath an elegant arch of brickwork. It swings easily on its hinges and will often slam shut like a sail caught in the wind if it is left open and unsecured, even for a moment. Its wood is untreated and is nibbled by wasps in the summer, collecting cellulose pulp to make their nests. Come September, their colonies are fading and you are more likely to come across solitary queen wasps searching for a winter roost. The path beyond the door leads past the rear entrance of the former gardener's house (previously the home of George and Dolly Smith) and on round the corner to the yard, past the large *Rosa banksiae*. Within the walls, the door opens on to the long orbital gravel path that circumnavigates the four quarters of garden. This was our velodrome as children. My favourite speedway bike, a red and white number with grey pneumatic tyres, barely reaches the height of my knees as an adult. We would race around the paths in the summer and autumn evenings, throwing up gravel on the sharper corners, bouncing over a manhole cover near Charlie's old shed.

Moving clockwise, along the south side of the garden, the next entrance is the hand-wrought iron gate made by S C Pearce & Sons of Bredfield. This was commissioned to celebrate my grandparents' silver wedding anniversary. On the outer side of the wall a young *Cotoneaster frigidus* forms a natural archway, fringed by a fragrant tangle of honeysuckle and the dark purple rose La Reine des Violettes. Inside the garden, two holly trees stand like sentries on either side of the path behind low box hedging.

Continuing on the orbital path in a clockwise direction takes you past a patch of *Primula denticulata* and primroses, a disused underground boiler, various vegetable patches, the compost heaps, a run of domesticated blackberries, Lord Derby, some gages and a large fig tree. Beyond these, next to a clump of lemon verbena, is the third entrance to the garden – the door to the gardener's bothy. This is tucked into the wall next to the chilli house. The neatly glazed door opens into a tiny sitting room, complete with a Victorian iron grate and open fire. Previously comprising an old earth closet (which sustained "her Ladyship's celery" in the 1920s), a derelict bedroom and tiny sitting room, the bothy was restored in 2007 and is now used as a small studio or retreat. Recent residents have included the painter Ffiona Lewis, sculptor Sarah Pirkis and Bulgarian icon painter Marchela Dimitrova, who has been researching the early saints of Suffolk and Ireland. (Suffolk was once nicknamed "silly Suffolk" from the Anglo-Saxon word "seilig" meaning "saintly". There were many strong links between the Anglo-Saxon and Celtic churches, through the conversions and teachings of St Fursey, St Botolph, St Audrey, St Felix and St Cedd, among many others.) Just as Ronald Blythe once sat in the garden to

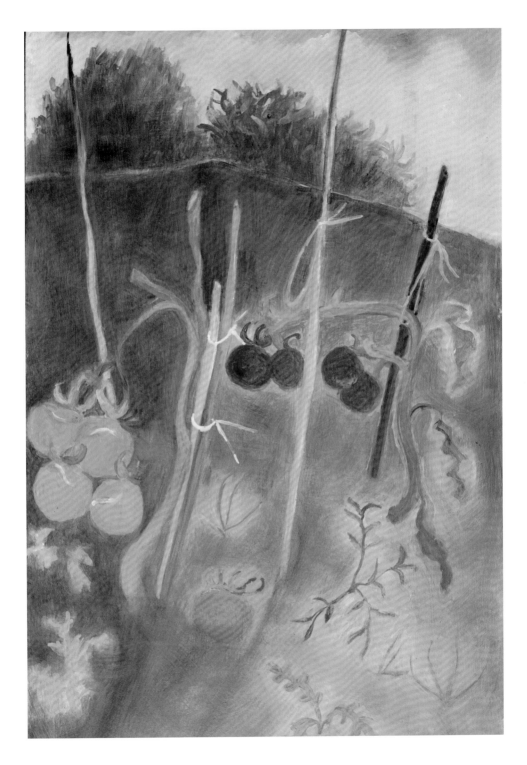

compose his own thoughts, the bothy has become a temporary home to new generations of artists and writers.

The final door is the oldest. Weather-beaten and heavy on its hinges, it stands at the north end of the main north-south promenade, opposite the wrought iron silver wedding gate. With the peach house and vine house on either side, it gives direct access to the potting shed and barrow store. As such, it is the main thoroughfare for daily activities in the garden, often left hooked open during the day – but *never* at night, lest rabbits or muntjac get in.

These four entrances are in constant use by visitors and workers in the garden. The cycle of activity is mirrored in the movement of plants and produce into and out of the garden. Seeds, saplings, cuttings and potted plants are brought in to be propagated; and seasonal produce is packed and taken away to be stored or eaten. Some is delivered to the house and apartments to feed friends and residents. Any surplus is dispatched in small quantities to Lawsons Delicatessen in Aldeburgh and Café 1885 at Snape Maltings.

At times, it feels as though the garden is a continuous play, in which the stories of plants that come in and out of it are intimately interwoven with the lives of the people who work there or pass through. The

Georgian chillies that my mother grows were originally a gift from Fitzroy MacLean, who had been given them at Tbilisi airport as a parting gift when he left the country in the early 1970s. The Slovenian beans were a present to my brother from the mayor of a small town in which he was staying while studying local architecture in the 1990s. A beautiful crab apple (*Malus hupehensis*), which now towers over the garden wall by the shrubberies, was brought back by Jock Cranbrook from the trip that he made to the Burmese-Tibetan border in 1931 with Kingdon Ward. It is covered each spring in a cloud of snowy blossom, which, by September, has usually grown into a heavy crop of tart, marble-sized bright scarlet crab apples.

Other seeds have been less successful. The seeds of a Bornean aubergine germinated and grew vigorously, covering its shoots with stiff two-inch spines, but refused to flower and set fruit. My mother's patience lasted about six months. Cherry tomato seeds that I retrieved from a plant growing in a drain outside my Godfather's garden in the Kelabit Highlands also grew prolifically, and even set fruit. But they looked curiously familiar to European commercial varieties – which may have been explained when my father had vague recollections of taking a packet of tomato seeds with him on a visit a few decades previously. Most peculiar of all was a trip my brother Argus made to Mount Athos, again on an architectural visit. He had heard tales of famous beans being grown there and asked a Guest Master if this was true and where the seeds came from. The Guest Master answered that he did grow beans and that he had a brother who sent him packets of beans from England - from a small town called Saxmundham in Suffolk. This is about five miles from Great Glemham. So if you want to try some really good beans, the answer may be to head to Saxmundham High Street and possibly to B C Fisher's, a small traditional hardware store and now the only shop on the High Street that sells packets of vegetable seeds. If they are good enough for Mount Athos, they are certainly good enough for the gardens of Suffolk!

Note: Appendix II ~ Growing Food for the House includes a comprehensive list of seed suppliers used for the garden at Great Glemham.

Glemham Aubergines & Peppers

Tilly Gathorne-Hardy

Several varieties of aubergine are grown in the Great Glemham garden, both indoors and outdoors. If the summer is hot, the outdoor ones do best. The most reliable and prolific varieties are Moneymaker and Violetta di Lunga, but these are supplemented by a few striped Listada di Gandia and the white Tonda Bianca.

Our friend Paddy Sutton, the Swedish/Irish photographer, once worked as a chef in Tuscany and serves this dish as a starter – but it is very filling and enough for a light lunch. The eye-popping Middle Eastern colours contrast wonderfully well with the yoghurt, like jewels on snow. Paddy brushes each piece of aubergine with oil, using a pastry brush. If this sounds too fiddly, we've found that you can jiggle them round in the pan and get pretty much the same result. The peppers are our own addition, thanks to the abundance of ruby-red beauties in the Glemham greenhouses – and even outdoors. We usually serve them stuffed into pitta breads; but they are equally delicious with couscous or stirred into bulgar wheat.

3 large aubergines
4 red peppers
Olive oil
1 pomegranate with its seeds knocked out
For the sauce:
225g of plain yoghurt
1 clove of crushed garlic
The juice of 1 lemon
A pinch of saffron
Ground black pepper and salt
A large handful of basil

Prepare the yoghurt sauce first, as it needs a few hours to settle and let the flavours intensify. Put the saffron strands into a small cup and pour in two centimetres of boiling water. Leave to steep for 10 minutes. Crush the garlic clove, squeeze the lemon juice and add to the yoghurt. Pour in the saffron liquid, including the strands, and stir. Cover and leave in the fridge for a few hours. Chop the aubergines into three-centimetre cubes. De-seed the peppers and cut into strips. Place them all in a roasting pan and lightly brush with olive oil, salt and ground black pepper. Roast on a high heat for 40 minutes, turning every 15 minutes. Spread the vegetables on a dish, drizzle them with the yoghurt sauce, scatter the pomegranate seeds and finish with a sprinkling of chopped basil leaves.

Squash
David Grimwood

Beautiful, beautiful squash, pumpkin and marrow – all splendid with autumn colours and fit for roasting with strong flavours: garlic, rosemary, orange-scented thyme, and wondrous Suffolk honey. Very good roasted with Alde Valley Lamb or mutton – or a brace of teal, plump from gleaning autumn barley stubbles.

1 winter squash
Hill Farm rapeseed oil
Herbs as suggested above
Sea salt
Cracked black pepper

Dice the squash to a convenient size, removing the seeds, any pith and the tough skin. Put in a roasting pan and drizzle with the rapeseed oil plus the herbs, sea salt and cracked black pepper to taste. Cook in a medium oven. Add the honey when the squash is nearly cooked (ie, beginning to feel tender when pricked with a skewer). If the honey is included too early it becomes dark, treacly and bitter to taste. Cook until tender and eat with splendour.

The Weight of Two Eggs
Coney Jarvis/Caroline Cranbrook

This easy recipe works well with any fruit. It was given to us by my mother, Coney Jarvis, who learned it from her mother, Aileen Meade.

2 eggs
Sugar
Self-raising flour
Butter
Fresh fruit
Water
A small amount of additional sugar

Weigh the eggs and then use the same weight for the sugar, flour and butter. Cream the butter and sugar and then beat in the eggs and flour. Fill a pie dish two thirds full with fruit (eg, halved plums or damsons, peeled and diced pears or apples). Add sugar to taste and a little water to moisten. (Not much is needed since the fruit will produce quite a lot of liquid.) Spread the mixture evenly over the fruit and cook in a moderate oven at 180C for 35-40 minutes. It is best eaten hot but the left-overs are good cold.

October

*Beans and their leaves hang
forlorn on their strings.*

*Inside the greenhouse – a
wonderful array of golds and
white – the squashes are all
lined up – and the piggies –
those too big green squashes.*

Two men in pink among the vegetables.
Tessa Newcomb

This page: Sad little hen

October

Garden Notes

Harvest last of tomatoes and courgettes. Remove tomato plants that have finished fruiting. Bundle up stakes. Trim and de-leaf vines to expose bunches of grapes. Sow lettuce seeds. Pick beans for drying. Clean mowers. Rake up fallen apples and pears in fruit cage. Move geraniums from the yard back to greenhouse. Harvest squashes and set out on benches in the vine house. Harvest quince. Start picking dried runner beans for seed and winter stores. Rake up leaves from garden paths and fruit cage. Pick tomatilloes and dig up plants. Prune blackberry bush against the garden wall. Trim yew hedges. Move chrysanthemums to porch. Dig over and clear chilli house to prepare for winter lettuces. Harvest chestnuts from car park tree.

A FEW YEARS AGO an old bathing hut * stood on the concrete perimeter track of Parham Airfield above Great Glemham village. It was nine miles inland and a hundred feet above sea level: far from the reach of the North Sea tides. Quite how it came to be there is a mystery, but it had found a second life as a café or eating house of sorts, being used by men working at a nearby pig farm for their "eightses" – an early riser's elevenses. The word is another crumb of a rich local dialect that still existed in pockets of rural Suffolk until two or three decades ago, but which has now largely disappeared. The vocabulary for snacks reflected the patterns and timetables of the working day. "Snaps", "baits", "snatches" and "foorzes" were all morsels of food, while "whets" were

---

* I learned the story of the bathing hut from David Creed in Great Glemham, a long-time resident and stalwart in the community. Ark-like in its location on Parham Airfield, the hut was later moved to the garden of a cottage near Great Glemham church. It still exists, although I think it has become a case of "my grandfather's axe". "My grandfather had an axe which he left to my father. My father broke its head. He had it replaced and gave the axe to me. I broke the handle and, when it is repaired, I'll pass it to my son. For it is my grandfather's axe – and cannot be thrown away ... ."

liquid refreshment. "Nunshens", or "noonins", were a bit more substantial and "bevers" were an afternoon food-stop for the harvest workers in autumn. As their names suggest, nunshens and noonins were a midday meal, while foorzes were a tea break.

It seems that many of these words and the food traditions that went with them have slipped away as the combustion engine replaced both the plough team and human muscle power on the land. Machines need less refreshment and, unless they overheat, have no need to stop until a job is done – or the driver needs a rest. The arrival of the internal combustion engine, besides leading to the progressive elimination of most heavy horse work on farms – ploughing, rolling, harrowing, cultivating, weeding, harvesting, threshing, carting and winching of timber – also extinguished many manual jobs about the farm and garden. As engines became more and more compact, hand tools for a huge range of activities were replaced by small portable machines. Digging, cultivating, sowing, hoeing, scything, hedging, ditching, pruning and tree-felling all became much easier and faster. While this shift has made life much easier and more comfortable for those who are still left working on the land or in gardens, it has also led to a steady loss of jobs and knowledge.

One of the greatest upheavals in farming practices was the transition from horse power to tractors. Horsemen, who had been at the top of farmyard hierarchies, suddenly found themselves redundant, their horses sold or shot. Their special knowledge of horse husbandry, medicines and magical potions, cherished and handed down over centuries, became useless almost overnight and was soon forgotten. The rating of tractor and other vehicle engines in terms of horsepower is a poignant reminder of this former age, as are the dashboards, glove boxes and running boards of cars – you will find them on any smart horse-drawn carriage. With less company in the field – often none – and no draught animals to look after, farming has become both busier and more solitary. There is hardly anybody left to share a round of eightses, noonshuns and baits. The only exception to this is perhaps bevers, for harvest is still a communal activity. It requires a combine, tractors and trailers, balers and sometimes even the plough to be operating in close co-ordination. If the weather is clement and the harvest is good, there is still time for a shared snack. The practice survives, even if the name has been lost or discarded.

This pattern has been mimicked in the kitchen garden. Machines have again tended to replace people, albeit in a less obvious or dramatic way. A quick look around the potting shed reveals the changes. All manner of shears – long handled, angled, straight-headed and short-handled – lie in the loosest drawer of the tall chest by the door or hang

from nails in the wall. Oiled, cleaned and ready for use, they rarely leave the shed now: the slow-paced, wrist-jarring snap of un-cushioned hand shears has been overtaken by the rapid chatter of electric hedge clippers, or the fuming roar of the petrol version. Box hedges and laurel bushes which once took several people a week or more to trim can now be done in a few days. Lines of spades and forks, again well-oiled, see more action, but less than in previous years. The gardener's art of trenching or double-digging, which turns soil and manure over to a depth of up to eighteen inches, has

been partly replaced by petrol-driven rotavators. A choice of attachments allows the vegetable beds to be turned, ploughed and furrowed. Long-handled slashers and scythes hanging among wooden rakes at the further end of the potting shed now see only occasional outings. Heavy patches of brambles or scrub in the shrubberies which would in the past have been attacked at the roots with a slasher, swung golfing-style, are now shredded by the toothed metal disc of a brush-cutter or heavy-duty strimmer. Fitted with a bright nylon cord, it laps it laps up long grass and nettles, coating one's legs with a sticky blast of shredded stems. Most of the lawns are now cut by a ride-on Stiga mower. A variety of Ransomes and two small manual mowers gather cobwebs in the sheds. The manual mowers needed two men to operate them – one pulling, the other pushing. A fearsome five foot long, flat-deck mower with a towed seat is parked nearby. It was driven by a neighbour, Cliff Rainer, in the 1970s, and once let loose a blade from its gaping front. The piece of metal sheared off its bolts and flew out from the front of the mower at phenomenal speed. With a whizzing "thunk", it spun across the lawn and struck a mulberry tree, embedding itself in the trunk.

The march of machines has speeded up many jobs on the farm and in the garden. On the farm, it has also extended the working day – it is not uncommon now to see tractors and harvesters of many sorts humming away late into the night. In the kitchen garden, the daily rhythm is still very much eight till half four, with a mid-day break – an old fashioned noonshens, now known by another name. By the middle of October both farmland and garden are quietening down after the rush of late summer. In a mild year, the last outdoor squashes, aubergines, peppers, chillies and tomatoes are gathered in, together with the fruits and nuts of autumn. There is a sense of the year changing, with occasional south-westerly storms pulling at the leaves on the taller trees in the shrubberies. More foods go into the house for preserving and pickling. Chestnuts fall from two trees, mother and daughter, near the entrance to the stable yard. The older tree rises out of a huge bole of living wood and has good-sized fruit. If the summer and early autumn are dry, there is usually only one edible nut in each velvet-lined, prickly capsule – and this often wormy. If the weather has been mild and damp, there may be one good nut and one or two smaller ones. Very occasionally, both August and September are wet and there is a mast year: every fruit has three huge nuts in it, all healthy. 2010 was like this. The smaller sweet chestnut was planted as a seed by Charlie Chandler. He used to sit under it popping peas and shelling broad beans. A small grove of blackcurrant bushes

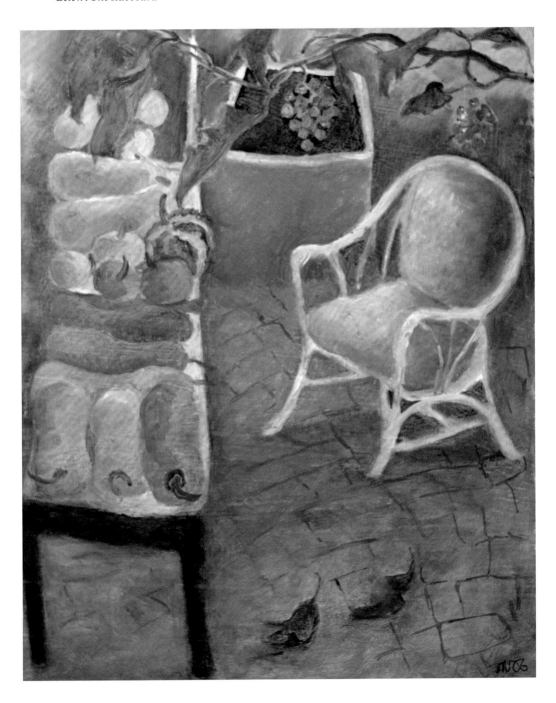

nearby have become spindly as the chestnut has grown tall and spread. It dropped its first crop of large nuts in 2011. The leaves of both trees begin to change colour soon after, falling towards the end of October. On the ground, damp and darkening as the pigments within them change, the fallen leaves assume the colour and appearance of smoked kippers.

October is traditionally the month of Harvest Home in both the garden and on the farm. Bunches of the best Muscat and Hamburg grapes are sent to the village church for the Harvest Festival service. Every parish in the Alde River Benefice holds a service, often with an informal supper as well. In Great Glemham, Michael Salter keeps a sheaf of wheat from the harvest fields to go into the church for the Harvest Festival. The congregation and visitors bring food to share for a communal meal after the service. In a world in which so much food is still available (though, tragically, often very poorly shared and distributed) and in which so much produce is also rejected, lost or wasted, it feels important to treasure the simple gift of existence and to share the abundance that is around us. Many places on the planet struggle with an inch or two of topsoil or less. In the sandy loams and meadowlands of Suffolk – and in the kitchen garden – the topsoil is sometimes more than a foot deep. This is a luxury that should not be overlooked or lost. (I remember once digging rushes out of pastures on a hillside overlooking the Atlantic ocean in Co Kerry in Ireland and being shocked at the rich black soil that lay hidden beneath the rough pasture. So much effort had obviously gone into the making of the land. The fields were protected by dry stone walls and dotted with large piles of pebbles and shale, all picked by hand from the fields. Here and there were the remains of "crazy beds", once fertilized with seaweed gathered from the rocky shore below. There was so much fertility still left in the once carefully tended soil, yet it was slipping back to gorse and scrub.)

For many years a farm Harvest Supper was also held at Glemham House. This continued into the late 1990s. My parents would prepare a meal for 25 to 30 guests (employees, friends and family) serving ham, pies, terrines, vegetables and puddings. Apart from pork, poultry, beef and dairy ingredients, almost everything on the table came from the kitchen garden. Charlie Denny would make a corn dolly from the last of the harvest's wheat or barley stems and Peter Plant, who lived in a caravan behind the village pub, would play a few tunes on his squeezebox. The Harvest Supper came to an end when our family moved to contract farming in 2000, but autumn celebrations reappeared a few years later with a series of autumnal food projects held in the barns at White House Farm. These have focused on the importance of livestock farming in the Alde Valley, with small exhibitions, farmyard BBQs and wild food walks. These featured in the Channel 4 series *Wild Gourmets*. The presenters Guy Grieves and Thomasina Miers (who has gone on to create the *Wahaca* chain of restaurants) camped for five days at the edge of Backhousepond Covert. The drop toilet they left behind has joined WWII army trenches, sandpits and old earth boundary ditches as part of the local woodland archaeology.

Tsiala's Churchkhela

Natalia Wilkinson

1 litre of white or pink grape juice
30 walnuts
1 cup of sugar
1 1/4 cups of plain white flour
A heavy duty thread

Cut each walnut into four pieces. Thread a large needle with a 40cm length of heavy duty cotton cord. Make a knot. Thread twenty four pieces of walnut on to the cotton, tying a large loop at the loose end. Repeat this process until you have used up all the walnuts.

Mix approximately 300ml of grape juice (home made or bought-in) with 1 1/4 cups of flour. Stir to remove lumps. In a large saucepan pour the remainder of the juice. Add one cup of sugar and bring it to the boil. Then quickly add the porridge-like mix of flour and juice into the boiling syrup, whisking constantly so that no lumps are formed. Leave to boil at a low heat for about 25 minutes. Dip the threaded nuts into the hot porridge mixture. Hang the threads over paper to dry for 15 minutes. Repeat the dipping process two or three times, or until the walnuts are fully covered and coated. Leave to dry for three to four days or until the strands are no longer sticky to touch.

Beetroot & Walnuts

Caroline Cranbrook

The following recipe comes from Georgia and is basically a vegetable puree/mixture (phkali) to which ground walnuts and herbs (bazha) are added. The combination is just as successful with beetroot as with spinach, leeks, courgettes and even mushrooms. Bazha goes well with chicken, fish or game.

450g beetroot
Half a cup of shelled walnuts
3 garlic cloves
Handful of chopped coriander leaves
Handful of chopped parsley
Handful of chopped summer savory or thyme
Ground black pepper and ½ tsp salt
½ tsp chilli powder
½ tsp ground coriander
2 tsp vinegar
A little chicken stock

Bake the unpeeled beetroot for about an hour at 190 C until tender. Combine walnuts, garlic, pepper and salt in food processor. Add fresh herbs and continue to blend until it forms a paste. Peel the beetroot and grate coarsely into a bowl. Add the walnut paste and remaining ingredients; start with a little vinegar and add more according to taste. Mix by hand. Moisten with stock if necessary.

Cabbage with Ginger & Chilli

Caroline Cranbrook

Cabbage is a great standby throughout the year, but especially in winter. The following recipe is based on a Malaysian method, which I learned during my first years of marriage when we lived on the edge of the jungle near Gombak, north of Kuala Lumpur.

1 white cabbage
2-3 tbs olive oil
2 cloves of garlic
1 hot chilli
1 "thumb" of ginger
Ground black pepper and salt
Sprinkling of black mustard seed
Coconut milk or ordinary milk

Crush or pound in a mortar the chilli, garlic and ginger. Then fry lightly in the olive oil in a large saucepan. Before the garlic browns, add the finely chopped cabbage. Stir well, cover and cook over a low heat for a few minutes. Stir and then add about 250ml of coconut milk or ordinary milk. Stir again, cover and cook for fifteen to twenty minutes or longer until the cabbage is soft, checking from time to time that there is enough liquid. Finish with seasoning and a sprinkling of black mustard seed.

Caramelised Crescents of Quince

Flora Gathorne-Hardy

The quince has a very ancient history and is thought to be the golden apple of fairy tale and myth, sacred to the Greek goddess Aphrodite. Its scented, pear-shaped golden fruit appear in autumn, bright beacons among the turning leaves. This recipe is a simple alternative to membrillo quince cheese and the chewy crescents can be enjoyed on their own, or added to complement a cake or other puddings, or served with cheese.

Ripe quinces
Sweet syrup (concentrated apple juice,
*   honey or agave syrup)*
A dash of Japanese Umeshu (a salted
*   plum vinegar) or a pinch of salt*

Wash the fruit and cut into quarters, leaving the peel on. Remove the core and cut lengthways into thin 2-3mm slices to create crescents. Put about 1 tablespoon of syrup for each quince and a few splashes of Umeshu (or a pinch of salt) into a bowl. You will need enough syrup to coat the slices generously. Oil a baking tray and lay out the slices evenly. Bake in a low oven for 1-1 ½ hours or until golden brown and glistening.

November

A downfall of leaves.
The effect of a silent gust
of wind.

A dropped chilli.
A passing helicopter.

Stuart's red hat. Pruning
roses against a wall. His
shiny ladder in the same
place as last year.
Tessa Newcomb

This page: Spirals

158

November

Garden Notes

Weed asparagus beds. Prepare beds in fruit cage for new raspberry varieties. Fork round and tidy Italian artichokes. Dig over ends of asparagus beds. Clear late sweetcorn plants and feed to sheep. Check apple store. Dig over and spread muck on vegetable beds in front of the old greenhouses. Trim and train plum trees against the garden wall. Pick medlars. Clear runner bean haulm from fruit cage and plastic mesh. Prepare and plant garlic. Sow broad beans and sweet peas. Send carrots and potatoes to the house. Start pruning roses along the main herbaceous borders in the garden. Start pruning gooseberries, raspberries, currants and apple trees in the fruit cage.

WITH THE HARVEST celebrations of October already a memory, the weather of November brings with it the need to be ready both for the coming winter and a more distant spring. Just as February is the month in which building repairs are reviewed for the warmer months of June, July and August, so November is the time to start planning what vegetables will go where in the garden in the following year.

Some plants are quite happy to stay in one spot year after year. Globe artichokes, asparagus, rhubarb and soft fruits, such as raspberries, gooseberries and currants, will thrive in their own particular corner of the garden – provided they are weeded and well-tended with manure and wood ash. But other plants – the cabbage family, peas, beans, tomatoes, potatoes and other root crops – need to be rotated. This is to avoid the build-up of root pests and other bugs that prey on the shoots or fruits. There is the added complexity that some varieties of vegetables do not grow well if they follow on after another, and others fare better if they have companion plants. For past generations of gardeners, this was practical folklore, passed carefully down from head gardeners to understudies and from one gardener to another. At first, this planning is simply a matter of deciding which type of vegetable is allocated to the different segments of the walled garden, mapped on a large board kept by Chris in the potting shed. More detailed decisions about which particular varieties to keep and which to replace with new stock come later in the winter. My mother usually does her seed orders early in the new year, sifting through catalogues, checking prices and provenance, noting orders and listing all purchases in her seed books, now a library of pocket books that spans 40 years.

With temperatures falling and the days shortening, it is time to start taking down last season's structures. As the stage-set for the previous summer's production is slowly dismantled, the bare walls and soil of the garden become exposed once again. The pea cage disappears. The last of the regimented lines of canes that supported tomatoes, peas and beans are pulled up, brushed down and packed away. Remains of squash plants and sweetcorn, now draped over the ground or standing brown, damp and tattered, are gathered into barrows. Any parts that are still green are fed to the sheep and chickens. The rest is composted. Dried out stems of climbing beans that have become enmeshed in the walls of the fruit cage are carefully disentangled.

The removal of old plant growth from the vegetable beds creates clear ground again and space to start the annual cycle of digging in muck from outside. This is a major undertaking. Ten to fifteen tons of farmyard manure are brought in by trailer and dumped by the firewood store a hundred yards from the potting shed entrance. This is broken down into barrow loads, which are wheeled or towed into the garden and up-ended into a regular pattern of heaps on the four quarters of vegetable beds. These are then spread and dug in, patch by patch, pile by pile. It is a long, hard process, but good muck and a well-aerated free-draining seed bed with weeds well buried will underpin next year's production.

Around the walls, climbing roses and trained fruit trees receive a trimming. Chris (and sometimes my father) are often to be seen atop a wide aluminium ladder, secateurs in hand – or occasionally as a head appearing over the top of the wall. Some of the fruit trees, such as the figs, damson and Victoria plum, are left alone, pruned only every few years. Others, such as the gages, peaches, apricot, nectarine and vines – together with the apples and pears in the fruit cage - are trimmed each year. This encourages fruiting, but also reflects their more constrained growing environments.

In the vine house, most of the Muscat and Hamburg grapes have been picked. A few bunches of strawberry grapes usually remain, gathering a rich sweetness as the leaves about them slowly fade to yellow, detach and drop, abandoning the spaces in which they have been intercepting sunlight for the past few months. Two pairs of scissors made from soft, old fashioned iron each hang from a nail by one finger hole on the white-washed wall along the back to the greenhouse. They look like strange metallic birds, beaks open, ready to snip. Nearby, a broken thermometer gauge fails to record the temperature. But it too has become part of the furniture of the vine house. On the floor, laid out on sacks, and on the tops of three tables (a sun-bleached pine workbench, a metal-rimmed formica cabinet and an old lead-covered work bench) are piles of pumpkins and squashes. They are all in transit, brought under cover to protect them from the early frosts of winter. The vine house in November consequently has the feeling of a waiting room. The smaller varieties of squashes are arranged in groups on the table tops. The larger varieties, including the sinuous Tromba d'Albenga and Serpente di Sicilia, lie in tangled piles on the ground and on top of the old steam pipes. The Gourds of Napoli – my mother's "green pigs" – have a space all of their own. They are so heavy that they have to be moved in and out of the greenhouse in a metal cart or wheel barrow. Any that succumb to frosts are chopped up and fed to the chickens as a carotene-rich meal.

Most of the chickens now live in the "stickhouse" – an old poplar-

clad shed that stands near the edge of the park in the shrubberies. When I was a child, it housed a small horse-drawn, hand-pumped fire engine. This was given to the Ipswich Fire Service and the hut has since been home to generations of Silver Spangled Hamburgs and Andalucian chickens. Other groups of Buff Cochins, Partridge Cochins, Polish bantams and even a Silkie have dwindled away over the years as the number of foxes has increased. Sadly, it is now impossible to let the hens roam free – they all live inside fenced runs, unless let out under close supervision. A small group of grey Araucana bantams survive in a pen on the other side of the walled garden from the stickhouse – now a solitary enclave in a part of the garden that they used to share with a large group of feathery-footed Buff Cochins. The Cochins' pen now stands abandoned overlooking Crabbe's hill like a Roman outpost on a North Sea shore.

November is also the month in which the remainder of the bean crop comes into the house. Climbing beans (Pea Bean, Borlotti, Slovenian, Hungarian, Cherokee and Gigantes varieties) were picked as individual pods in September and have already been drying for two months on wicker trays in the main house. Dwarf bean plants that were uprooted at the same time have been drying upside down wherever there is an airy, dry space in the garden – from wires in the vine house, from the rungs of ladders stored in the rafters of the barrow store or from beams in the roof of a lean-to shed next to the old boiler room. They are usually dry by the middle of November. The pods are then stripped off and taken indoors to join the climbing beans. Once in the house, they are spread out on rattan winnowing trays from Sarawak (sourced from Pesta Nukenen* and basket makers in Pa Umor village) and left to dry for a further two or three weeks. At the end of this period they are finally shelled, dried again and then placed for storage in old sweet jars – a leftover from the days in which there was still a shop on the village Street.

---

* Pesta Nukenen (The Bario and Kelabit Highlands Food and Cultural Festival) is the sister event of The Alde Valley Spring Festival. Founded by members of the Kelabit Highlands community in 2006, it gained financial independence from the Spring Festival in 2009. It is managed by the Kelabit Highlands Kaum Ibu women's group, with support from the Council of Elders, village headmen, BELIA youth group, Rurum Kelabit Sarawak, sponsors from the community and the UK, including the Worshipful Company of Water Conservators.

Beetroot Soup

Marcia Blakenham & Stephanie Bullard

Borscht soup is delicious but I like this recipe even better. It is not necessary to roast the beetroots first (rather than boiling), but roasting them improves their flavour.

4 large or 6 small beetroots
1 large onion
1 large potato
1.5 litres good chicken stock
1 tbs cream
½ tsp horseradish sauce
Chopped dill
Pepper
Salt to taste

Roast the beetroot for about 1½ hours in a hot oven until soft. Fry the chopped onion until transparent in a little butter, add the chopped potato and soften that a bit too. Add the chicken stock and bring back to a simmer. Skin the beetroot, slice it and add it to the pot. Simmer altogether until soft. Add the horseradish, seasoning and cream. Put it all in a blender and zap it smooth. Return to the saucepan and reheat. Before serving, add lemon juice and a bit of finely chopped dill if you have it.

Sour Cabbage

Miche Fabre Lewin

Fermented food needs no fuels, no cooking and no particular climate. Fermentation is an ancient, world-wide tradition of preserving seasonal surpluses and rendering food safe to eat. Invite your friends to join in what can be a communal activity, harnessing bio-diversity in the kitchen.

1 medium-sized cabbage (red, green or
*   white)*
Sea salt or rock salt

Quarter the cabbage. Cutting diagonally, remove the central core of each quarter. Finely slice the cabbage length-wise into shreds. Add one generous tablespoon of salt per cabbage and, with your hands, massage the salt through the shredded cabbage until it softens and becomes moist and shiny. The salt and the handling begin to break down the cell walls and attract airborne micro-organisms, which begin the lactic fermentation. When all the cabbage is salted, take a clean, wide-topped, sealable jar and begin packing handfuls of the cabbage tightly into it. Press each layer down evenly and firmly with your hands and the salted juices will start to rise above the layers. Keep

Char-grilled Partridge, Butternut Squash & Sage

Peter Harrison

putting on the pressure and continue packing the cabbage until you reach the top of the jar. At this stage, the juices will be completely covering the cabbage by at least two finger-widths and flowing over the top. Fermentation takes place in the warmth of the kitchen and in a visible place. Put your jar on a plate with a rim to catch excess salted water. Make a weight with a smaller jar filled with water that fits easily within the mouth of the cabbage jar, making sure you leave a space for air. Press down on this weight at least two or three times daily for seven to ten days. This is to keep the juices rising up and flowing out of the jar. Continue until no more bubbling, air-filled juice flows out. Once this drying out has happened, it is time to seal the jar. The length of fermentation will depend on the season and the warmth of your kitchen. As long as it remains sealed, the cabbage can be stored for months, gaining a sourer, more intense flavour.

Partridge lends itself really well to the charcoal barbecue.

1 partridge
1 large butternut squash
Sage leaves
Pepper and sea salt
Olive oil
For the Marinade

1 lemon (zest and juice)
2 cloves garlic
2 tbs sea salt
400 g plain Dijon mustard
2 tbs finely chopped flat parsley
400ml sunflower oil

Place all the ingredients for the marinade, apart from the oil, in a blender and "blitz", then slowly drizzle the oil in until combined. Prepare the partridge by removing the backbone, flattening open and scoring the breasts and thighs. Cover with the marinade, cling-film the bowl and leave in the fridge for one to two days. Barbecue the bird for 15-20 minutes, turning half way through. Peel, remove seeds and cut one large squash into small chunks. Make a foil "parcel" containing the squash, sage leaves, salt, pepper and a drizzle of olive oil and place on the barbecue for twenty minutes alongside the partridge. Serve the two together.

December

This is where it begins.
I'm witnessing the beginnings amongst
the remnants.
The birds are starting.
The year is turning into the next.

Hard nights – but these clear days – the sun gets through my trousers.

Bunches of mistletoe and smoke rising straight from the fires of the big
house.

The pond is nearly empty – all its geometry exposed.
This is my Burnt Norton.
I hear the "children in the shrubbery"
from another year.
I followed the bird – quick, quick.

Strong sun but going fast.
Geese in the parkland. Downy
feathers and molehills in the
grass. The old pony is by the cattle grid.
All gather as near as possible to
the big house to guard it and be fed.

Tessa Newcomb

This page: Hens on the first of December

December

Garden Notes

Fill firewood stores for the winter. Start digging and mucking all vegetable beds. Check and tidy fruit store. Set traps for mice. Finish pruning fruit trees. Start cleaning and oiling hand tools. Tie up winter covers for all outside taps and exposed pipe work. Start raking garden paths. Plant "Winter Density" lettuces in greenhouse. Take down vines. Plough potato area. Dig up old raspberry plants. Move chickens. Continue pruning roses around main house. Look after dogs. Set up stakes and netting for broccoli. Cut down daisies in front of house. Clear paths in herb garden. Check firewood and heating in the bothy. Collect earth from molehills for potting. Cut bamboos to be used as next year's garden canes. Top up bird feeders. Clear dead and fallen timber in shrubberies. Bonfires. Dig out spreading bamboo. Take carrots, potatoes, onions, shallots and garlic into the house from the apple store. Clear weeds from rhubarb patch and empty mature compost heaps. Prune vines. Plant new orchard and garden fruit trees. Cut holly, ivy and mistletoe to decorate the house. Christmas and New Year holidays.

DURING DECEMBER the potting shed comes into its own as the headquarters for garden activities. From the late dawns of mid-winter until early dusk and beyond, a light and an electric heater are often on, bringing a warm glow to the room. During dull, damp December weather, it serves as a place of retreat for tea breaks and noonshens between forays into the walled garden to work on a long list of winter jobs. Most of these revolve around cleaning the vegetable beds, borders and walls and, of course, digging in tons of muck. The lowering of the vines in the grape house is another important task. This usually takes several days. Each stem is carefully trimmed and released from the ties that hold it to a metal sub-frame built beneath the main timbers of the vine house (which was painstakingly repaired by craftsmen from Ashbocking Joinery in 2010). The main stems are then re-secured on longer loops of twine so that they hang well away from the glass. They remain suspended like this until early March.

If the weather becomes too cold for digging and pruning, work moves into the greenhouses or to the shrubberies. Here fallen branches and dead wood are cut up. Where leaves are particularly thick on the ground, they are raked up as compost or for burning. The combination of cold dank air and wood smoke from chimneys and bonfires is a signature of December. Chris and my father are often to be found tending fires or collecting wood. In the Dell, my father sometimes lights a series of small fires with his grandchildren, while Chris has one main bonfire site behind an orchard in a clearing amid some young beech trees. Although not endemic in Suffolk, beech trees grow well on the deep loam and chalky clay soils around the marl pit at the back of the garden. A few yards away, a larch and a Douglas fir tree are powering upwards. The Douglas has gained a lead and its top is already 60 or 70 feet above ground level, poking above the canopy of mature oak and beech trees. The larch has been slowed down by a long, sliding entanglement with a clump of *Clematis vitalba,* or Old Man's Beard. The sprawling stems of the latter are locked into a race against gravity as they try to reach the top of the larch before the tree's branches collapse under the weight of the climber's stem. For the time being, the climber's new shoots are growing upwards more quickly than the tree's branches are breaking off. At ground level, the larch stands in a strange-looking nest of its own fallen limbs and a large coil of Old Man's Beard. The sight reminds me of creepers in the forests of Borneo, which adopt all manner of contortions to pull themselves up into the tops of their host trees.

In the coldest winter weather, the potting shed becomes the place of final retreat. Hand tools await repairs, cleaning and oiling. If there are more than a few inches of snow, an old wooden snow plough is pulled out

and used to clear essential paths around the garden. At this time of year, most of the movements to the main house are focused on foods and fuel. Squashes, potatoes, onions, garlic, carrots, apples, sprouts, red cabbages, leeks and kales are ferried indoors by the barrowful or taken in recycled boxes to pubs and cafés. Firewood is moved from a large wood store near the stickhouse to a smaller store in the stable yard, or directly to the main house. The latter has limited central heating, relying instead on wood burning stoves and open fires. A continuous supply of firewood is consequently vital during the winter months. If fires go out, frost settles on the inside of the windows. In the bedrooms, warmth comes from hot water bottles and extra layers of blankets or thicker duvets. I remember when we were small, my brother, sister and I huddled like young birds in front an electric blower heater to dress for school, wriggling and jostling each other for a share of warm air. (This is the same heater into which I stuck a thermometer, with disastrous results.)

At the beginning of December the last of several wheelbarrows full of tall chrysanthemums are wheeled round to the front door of the main house. The plants have been tended throughout the summer and autumn in pots, in order to bring them into flower in time for Christmas. Once at the front door, they are carefully unloaded and carried into the porch and inner halls. The rich scent of the flowers, mixed with the chalky smell of cold limestone and damp earth, is redolent of deep winter.

As Christmas itself approaches, activities in the garden gather into a small mid-winter rush. Extra provisions are brought into the house from the apple store and vegetable beds – leeks, brussel sprouts, apples, onions, more potatoes and carrots. Mistletoe is cut from old apple trees in the kitchen garden – there are clumps in several trees and at least one apple is riddled with it. (Mistletoe roots sometimes seem to become systemic within a tree, suddenly pushing out new clumps of leaves and berries over the whole canopy, sucking out all the nutrients from the tree – we have lost one apple tree in this way, after a final huge crop of mistletoe.) Holly, ivy, box and pine branches are gathered from the shrubberies to hang above the paintings and doorways of the main house. Chickens are stocked up with food and water. Bird feeders are topped up. Presents are bought, cards written. Finally, a Christmas tree is selected from the shrubberies or a plantation of young conifers in the New Wood beyond the park. There is usually a discussion about how tall it should be, and whether to cut a split-topped one, which would leave better trees to grow on, or a good strong straight tree, which would look nicer. Usually, a compromise is reached and a tree is brought in that reaches 20 ft high. After the stump end has been squared up with a saw, the tree is set upright in a huge glazed bathing jar from Malaysia – my father's bath tub when he and my mother lived at Gombak near Kuala Lumpur. The trunk is secured by tying it to the wrought iron banisters of the long hall staircase with pieces of garden twine and the tree is then decorated with baubles, tinsel and candles.

Christmas and the following days are always marked HOLIDAY in the potting shed calendar. For the gardener Chris it is time for a well-earned break from the busy cycle of production, preparation and cleaning that characterises a year in the kitchen garden at Great Glemham – and I am sure in many thousands of other gardens around Britain. With the new year, activity will return: the sound of spade against earth, rake on gravel, secateurs on rose stems, cockerels calling in the shrubberies and the hourly chime of the stable yard clock.

The following paragraphs were among the words that Tessa wrote down and collected during the three years in which she drew and painted in the garden. She wrote them towards the end of the residency project and it seems fitting to bring them into the last chapter of the book.

> *"I see this walled garden as from a satellite. A circle of time is held within it while the rest of the world moves on. I have been made to feel part of the family with its extended members – many of them plants.*
>
> *"I have loved coming to this place. Everything feels as if it is done for me. It is a sanctuary because it is not mine, but mine to look at and then to be able to leave."*

Perhaps this is the secret that lies at the heart of garden: it is a play on a stage that has no beginning and no end. It is a world apart. Within the walls of the kitchen garden the activities of the seasons and the comings and goings of people and plants all roll into one. Growth and decay, preparation and harvest, food and compost all overlap; the roots or waste of one year become the shoots and growth of another. As one crop ripens, another is being planted and a third is being thinned or pruned, on its way to production. The month of December, which can at times seem like a narrowing tunnel or the end of the year, is in fact, as Tessa wrote, "*where it begins*". It is the low ebb of the year, from which all life returns.

Pheasant Casserole, Celeriac & Apple Mash

Peter Clark

30 g butter

2 tbs vegetable oil

4 pheasant breasts

1 red onion peeled and sliced

1 clove garlic, peeled and crushed

125g chopped streaky bacon

1-2 tbs plain flour

150 ml dry cider

450 ml chicken stock

1 tbs cider vinegar

1 sprig thyme

1 bay leaf

500g peeled and cubed potatoes

2 Bramley apples peeled, cored and
    chopped

500g peeled and chopped celeriac

1 tbs chopped parsley

2 tbs sour cream

Salt

Ground black pepper

Melt the butter and oil in a large saucepan, brown the pheasant breasts and remove on to a plate. Add the onion, garlic and bacon and cook for three to four minutes until the onion starts to soften. Stir in the flour and cook for a minute. Add the cider, stock, vinegar, thyme and bay leaf. Season well. Bring to the boil and replace the pheasant breasts. Turn down the heat so the liquid bubbles gently and cover. Cook for 20-30 minutes until the pheasant is done and the sauce has thickened. Don't overcook or the meat will dry out. Meanwhile, bring a large pan of salted water to the boil and add the potato, apple and celeriac cubes. Boil until tender, drain, add the parsley and cream and some ground black pepper. Mash until smooth and serve with the pheasant casserole.

Basic Dried Bean Stew

Caroline Cranbrook

Many old bean varieties are disappearing as vegetable growers start using the commercial ones. This is very sad since not only are the old varieties very attractive to look at and good to eat, but they almost always grow more vigorously and productively than those that come in packets. The largest are the enormous white Gigantes, grown all over southern Europe. Mine came from the Piazza delle Erbe, part of the magnificent and enormous food market in and around Padua's medieval Town Hall. This recipe is suitable for Gigantes and smaller varieties of dried beans.

Dried beans
Olive oil
Small onion
Garlic
Chilli
Ground black pepper
Salt

Soak the dried beans in plenty of water overnight – *this is essential*. Remove any damaged beans. Drain and put in a pan covered with cold water. Bring to the boil and cook rapidly for five to ten minutes. Drain again. Heat one to two tablespoons of olive oil in a pan. Sweat a small chopped onion, sliced garlic and half a sliced chilli (optional) in the oil for a few minutes, followed by the beans. Stir well and then add one pint or more of chicken stock so that the beans are well covered by an inch of liquid. Season with black pepper and add a bay leaf and chopped herbs, such as parsley, basil, marjoram, savory or thyme. Do not include any salt during cooking as it will make the beans hard. At this stage you can either cover and cook until tender (on top of the stove or in a moderate oven) or you can add other ingredients such as game, or poultry, or diced ham or a piece of ham hock with a tablespoonful of black treacle and a teaspoon of mustard powder. Check periodically to see that the beans are still covered in liquid. Add more stock as necessary. The length of cooking will depend on how fresh they are. This season's beans will cook within the hour; older ones may take two hours or more. Add salt to taste when the beans are done.

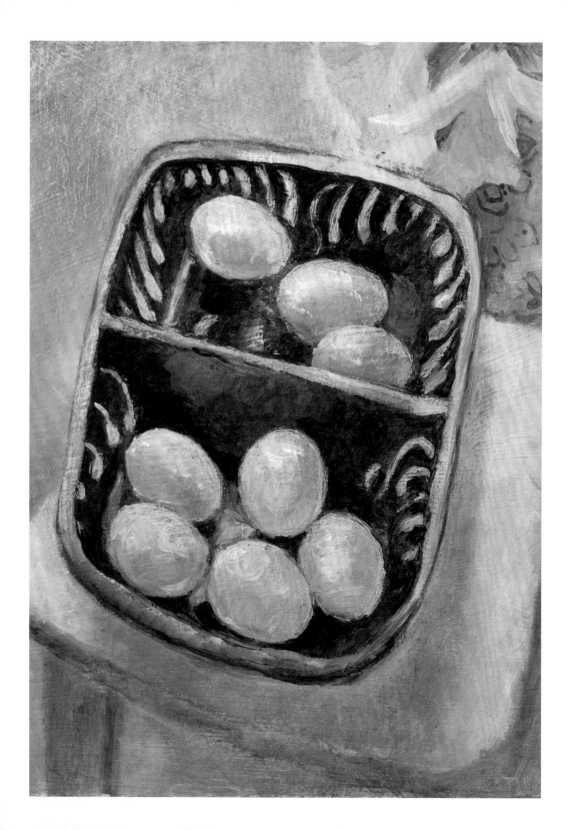

Appendix I:
Grateful Reflections
Gathorne Cranbrook

These are the names of some of the gardeners who have worked at Glemham House between 1913 and 2012. They (and many others) have helped to keep the walled garden alive, fertile and productive for the past century. This book and the present condition of the gardens are a tribute to their dedication.

Henry Syred (b. 1848 in Marlesford). Head gardener when the Cranbrook family first came to Great Glemham House in 1913.

William Syred (b. 1878). Son of Henry Syred.

Fred Brown. Moved from Great Glemham to Snape Priory in 1926 with Dorothy Cranbrook.

Mr Barrow. Worked in the gardens during the 1930s.

James Cobbin (b. 1904). One of 13 children of Peter Cobbin, whose family moved from one cottage to another in Great Glemham as his working life progressed. Another son, Edwin, was the youngest of 26 staff working at Glemham House in the early 1920s. Between 1923 and 1926 he was employed as the "backhouse boy", responsible for small jobs around the house and garden, including taking rubbish to nearby refuse pits in Backhousepond Covert.

Sydney E Paternoster (b. 1883). Son and brother of two family members who were longstanding gamekeepers at Great Glemham. He continued working in the garden through the 1930s.

Will Paternoster. Son of Sydney Paternoster. He helped his father in the garden for a short time and then as the estate gamekeeper.

Albert Easter.

Tom Eley. Son of Horace Eley, estate carpenter at Great Glemham, whose work included the 1931 restoration of Mosley's greenhouses. Tom worked in the garden for seven years through World War II, while the family lived at White House Farm. He retired to the Timber Yard in Great Glemham – part of the outbuildings of the former Great Glemham Hall (home of Suffolk poet George Crabbe between 1796 and 1801).

George Smith (born in Blaxhall). Gardener from the 1950s, living in the Harness Room flat on retirement. After George's death, his widow, "Dolly", remained here until leaving to join her son, Claude, in Woodbridge. George brought a "growing stone" to the garden.

Will Vice (b. 1897). Assistant gardener between 1957 and 1962. Born to a well-known Framlingham family, veteran of the British Indian Army, general farmworker, Will was seconded to the garden as assistant to George Smith until his retirement.

Mrs Julie Paternoster (née Budge). Julie came to Great Glemham as a wartime Land Army Girl, and married Walter Paternoster, son of Will, the gamekeeper. Julie kept the garden going single-handedly through the 1970s.

Charles Chandler. Gardener 1980-1998. Originally employed as lorry driver, Charlie came to Glemham House as a tenant of Flat 4. On losing his haulage job, he accepted the position as gardener and applied his dedication and skills to the task for almost two decades.

David Coles. Gardener 1998–2001. A young family man who came with experience from working in a garden centre. David carried on Charlie Chandler's work, managing the gardens well for three years, before returning to follow his own career in gardening.

Alan Sharpe. Gardener 2001 – 2005. Previously a farm worker, Alan applied enormous energy and dedication to the garden, bringing the land up to a high standard of fertility and cleanliness. He left the topiary "slug" and "snail" as his mementos.

Stewart Cousins. Gardener 2005-2008. Stewart came to Glemham House after retiring from a horticultural post at Otley College. He brought his skills and experience to the garden, until moving from the area in 2008.

Keith Saunders. Assistant gardener 2006-2008. Main gardener 2008-2009. An enthusiastic, self-taught young gardener, Keith joined us at 17 years old to assist Stewart. He ultimately decided to become self-employed, and is now doing well in the locality as a self-employed landscape gardener.

Robert Camp. Gardener 2009. Robert gave valued help in the garden for a short time, then found other work nearer his home.

Christopher Ellis. Gardener 2010-. A nephew of Tony Heffer, life-time tractor driver and part-time gamekeeper on the farm, Chris brought academic qualifications and skills in design, repairing the garden's dipping pond in 2011. He has also expanded his experience to the wide range of manual tasks in this large, historic garden, guided and supported by Caroline Cranbrook with occasional help from Alan Sharpe.

Left: Eggs in a slipware dish

Appendix II:
Growing Food for the House
Caroline Cranbrook

Here are some notes on the design of the gardens at Glemham House and the variety of foods grown in them, including a list of seed and plant suppliers used to stock the walled garden.

In the 1920s the kitchen garden was feeding not only the family and guests but also 20 or more servants (nanny, nursery maids, butler, housekeeper, footmen, parlour maid, housemaids, laundry maids, boot boy, grooms and possibly gardeners as well). This would have made a total of 30 or 40 people. A large proportion of the actual house as well as the staff would have been concerned with food, its preparation and particularly its preservation. In the part of the house which has now been made into flats there was a huge kitchen, scullery, pantry, still-room for making preserves, a store-room with slate-lined, sand-filled chests for keeping root vegetables in during the winter, and a cool room for milk, cream and butter. This list is probably incomplete: there may well have been other special activities and places that have been lost and of which there is no record.

Outdoors, an ice-house, game-larder, mushroom shed, vineries, peach houses, cucumber house, apple store, bothy, boiler rooms, barrow store and potting shed were all part of the original late Regency design. The potting shed was the engine-room of the whole enterprise. Indoors, the fruit would have been bottled and made into jams, jellies, pickles, syrups and cordials. Eggs would have been preserved in earthenware jars of water glass (sodium silicate); hams and home-cured bacon hung from large hooks in the kitchen ceiling; herbs dried in bunches; and many household products we take for granted, such as soap, would have been made at home. Every country house must have been like this; some smaller; some very much larger: but in all of them the garden and kitchen would have been working ceaselessly together, keeping up with the relentless cycle of the seasons, growing produce in season and out of season, fighting the weather, the pests and the diseases in order to feed the family and their servants throughout the year.

The kitchen today is much smaller but we still have an old-fashioned larder with large cupboards and slate-covered shelves, stacked with jars of dried beans, home-made fruit juices and syrups, chutneys and a library of jams and jellies, the oldest of which are useful for glazing ham. There is also a large chest freezer, filled with garden produce, game and our home-brand Alde Valley Lamb™. We are not as self-sufficient as our forebears, but we produce enough vegetables and fruit to feed our extended family and usually have a surplus to give away and sell to local pubs and delicatessen.

Manure, Water, Pests and Diseases

For nearly 200 years the garden's vegetable beds have received large annual helpings of manure, compost and leaf mould. Until the 1930s, this would have been supplemented by the contents of numerous privies and earth closets. All this organic fertilizer has resulted in a beautiful, fine, fertile soil. But this fertility is both a benefit and a drawback. It produces fantastic vegetables and fruit, but also copious weeds, the seed stock of which is constantly replenished by the annual trailer-loads of farmyard manure.

Suffolk is the driest county in England and water was and is a precious resource. By necessity, our ancestors were more frugal in the way they used it. At Great Glemham, the well provided water for the house, and roof water was stored in tanks for the laundry and for the garden and stables. A portion of the back park was used to feed water via field drains into the Green Pond at the back of the shrubberies, from where it was piped 3ft deep underground into the kitchen garden's central dipping pond and the stable yard – repairs to a wall in the yard in the 1970s punctured the pipework of a hitherto unknown water supply, causing water to spout from the masonry.

Gardening is always a constant battle against the animal kingdom and disease (conveniently seldom mentioned in the gardening media). Inside the garden walls we battle with mice, rats, voles, moles, grey squirrels, pigeons, pheasants, partridges, wasps, caterpillars, red spider, whitefly, greenfly and blackfly, while outside the kitchen garden rabbits and deer are an additional nuisance. Potato and tomato blight, honey fungus and botrytis (grey mould) on the grapes are our main disease problems. It is often a struggle. We spray only against blight in the potatoes and tomatoes, botrytis on the vines and caterpillars on the cabbages.

Rare and Unusual Fruit & Vegetables in the Garden
Apples
Examples of Lord Suffield, Lord Derby, D'Arcy Spice, Annie Elizabeth (with beautiful strongly coloured blossom and fruit) and Dr Harvey survive inside the kitchen garden. All these varieties are being revived by grafting. There is a poignant "graveyard" of lead labels

in the potting shed of long-dead varieties. It is puzzling that all the old apples are non-keeping cookers. Vast quantities must have been bottled in the past.

Artichokes

There is a thicket of three ancient varieties, one with such sharp prickles as to be a safety hazard when picking and eating it. All three have a much more delicate flavour than the modern varieties. We also grow a beautiful vigorous purple variety from Helmingham Hall and various ones from the Mediterranean which have small buds that can be eaten whole.

Sourcing Seeds & Growing Seedlings

I buy most of my seeds from commercial suppliers, apart from the dried beans and a few of the chillies. Some of the beans originally came from market stalls, bought mainly in Europe or given to me by family and friends. My first chilli was a present from the traveller Fitzroy Maclean in the 1970s on his return from Georgia. Its descendants survive, very recognisable and unchanged since I germinated the first seeds. It was Fitzoy's gift that started my interest in chillies and, indeed, in collecting unusual vegetable seeds. I am especially interested in old varieties and whenever abroad I always visit local markets, ironmongers and farming shops to see what I can find. The seeds sold in local markets by small farmers often turn out to be much more vigorous and healthier than those raised commercially. Unfortunately, these markets are changing and European regulations make this sort of sale impossible. I also collect roses and pelargoniums, many of which I have grown from cuttings. I have found several old varieties of roses in derelict cottage gardens, surviving in overgrown hedges. When I see these plants in the garden it is a nostalgic reminder to me of the places they came from and the people who gave them to me.

I sow seeds in small pots and start them in heated propagators, moving them out when they germinate. As soon as they are established with their first leaves, I transplant them into individual pots. Some of the more tender varieties, such as tomatoes, I then transplant again into larger containers, where they remain until the weather is warm enough for them to be planted out. I do not sow any seeds until February and March. Those sown earlier than this tend to damp off. Varieties, such as lettuce, I sow continuously every few weeks. As the weather becomes warmer, I stop using a propagator. All tomatoes and cucumbers are grown outside. Peppers, chillies and aubergines are mainly raised in an unheated greenhouse, but any surplus plants take their chance out of doors. If the summer is warm they do very well, but they are miserable in cold damp summers – and I have found that chillies need a hot summer to make them hot to taste.

Seed and Plant Suppliers

I pick and choose between the various suppliers, comparing prices and seed numbers. All of them supply a much larger range of seeds than I have mentioned and most sell vegetable and fruit plants, fruit bushes and garden sundries.

Peter Beales Roses, London Road, Attleborough, Norfolk NR17 1AY - 0845 481 0277. Very large selection of species and rose varieties.

Botanica, Chantry Farm, Eyke Road, Campsea Ashe, Woodbridge, Suffolk IP13 0PZ - 01728 747 113. Traditional nursery specialising in native British and home-grown fruit, hedgerow and shrubs. We are supporting the establishment of a "Crabbe Collection" with seeds from veteran trees at Great Glemham.

J.W. Boyce, Bush Pasture, Fordham, Cambs CB7 5JU - 01638 721158. Long-established seedsman, specialising in traditional vegetables and flowers, particularly pansies and old-fashioned sweet peas.

D.T. Brown, Western Aveue, Matrix Park, Chorley, Lancs PR7 7NB - 0845 3710532. Wide range of flower and vegetable seeds and potato varieties.

Crown Nursery, High Street, Ufford, Suffolk IP13 6EL 01394 460755. Good selections of soft fruit and fruit trees.

Franchi Seeds 1783, Unit 1A Phoenix Industrial Estate, Rosslyn Crescent, Harrow HA1 2SP - 0208 4275020. Specialising in Italian regional vegetable seeds, such as borlotti beans and squashes.

Marshalls, Alconbury Hill, Huntingdon, Cambs PE28 4HY - 01480 443390. Very good all round vegetable and flower seeds, onion sets and fruit bushes.

Mr Fothergill's, Kentford, Suffolk CB8 7QB - 08453 710518. Similar range to D.T. Brown.

Plants of Distinction, Abacus House, Station Yard, Needham Market, Suffolk IP6 8AS - 01449 721720. Specialises in old and unusual vegetable varieties.

Simpson's Seeds & Plants, The Walled Garden Nursery, Horningham, Warminster, Wiltshire BA12 7NQ - 01985 845004. Excellent for its wide range.

The Real Seed Catalogue, P O Box 18, Newport, Pembs SA65 0AA - 01239 821107. Heritage vegetable seeds.

The Walled Garden, Benhall, Saxmundham, Suffolk IP17 1JB - 01728 602510 Herbs, soft fruit, shrubs.

Woottens of Wenhaston, Halesworth, Suffolk IP19 9HD 01502 478 258. Excellent for pelargoniums and irises.

Appendix III:
Eat Your Weeds

Jason Gathorne-Hardy

Writing in the 16th century, the East Anglian farmer Thomas Tusser identified more than 70 vegetables and herbs for the kitchen garden in *Five Hundred Points of Good Husbandry*. Dorothy Hartley lists some of these in *Food in England* (p 396), including poppy, valerian, betony and sorrel. Today we have a much harsher definition of what constitutes a herb or vegetable and what is a weed. As a result, many interesting and nutritious shoots and roots end up on the compost heap or waste piles instead of on the plate. Below are a handful of weedy recipes for garden and hedgerow plants that can tastefully and economically broaden any diet. I have listed local ingredients from the Alde Valley for most of the recipes. These can be substituted by other edible wild or weedy foods where you live. *Wild Food* by Roger Phillips and *Food for Free* by Richard Mabey are both good reference books for identification of edible wild plants.

Dandelion Salad *Taraxacum officinale*
(Lion's Tooth, Blowball, Pittle Bed)

Ingredients
Approximately 25 young dandelion leaves – long tender green leaves from the middle of the rosettes are best
A good handful of young purple/green hawthorn shoots (see below)
5 free-range eggs
5 tablespoons of broken English walnuts
Cold-pressed Hill Farm rapeseed oil

Method
Wash dandelion leaves and hawthorn shoots, trimming ends where necessary. Dry and mix in a bowl. Hard boil the eggs. Cool in running water. Peel and cut each egg into four or five slices, either along their length or across. Lay sliced egg in rows on shallow platter or bowl, arranging dandelion leaves around the edge as a fringe. Add hawthorn shoots on top of the fringe. Sprinkle crumbled walnut pieces on top of the eggs, with a twist or two of coarse black pepper. Pour on a rapeseed dressing, mixed to your taste.

Elderflower Fritters *Sambucus nigra*
(Elderberry, Black Elder)

Ingredients
12 large elderflower heads. Take care to leave at least two inches of green stem at the base of each flower. The florets should be breaking bud and open. Avoid flower heads on which the florets are all still in bud (too young) or turning brown and falling off (too old).
Organic/local white flour
Free-range eggs
Sarawak black pepper
Greene King/Adnams Ale/Aspalls cider
Single or double cream
Demerara sugar
Sunflower oil

Method
With flour, eggs, ale/cider and a pinch of black pepper, prepare approximately 1 litre of light batter. Add 2 tablespoons of demerara sugar to the mix. Pour sunflower oil into a small/medium high sided saucepan until about 1½ inches deep. Turn on the heat, testing the oil with droplets of batter. When the droplets instantly bubble and fry, place flower heads in oil and cook one at a time. First, holding each flower by the tip of its stalk, dip the flower head in the batter, stirring it around until all the florets are covered. Still holding the tip of the stalk, remove the flower head from the batter, allow excess to run off for a moment or two and then carefully lower the head into the pan of hot oil. Leave it deep-frying until all the batter is crisp and beginning to turn golden. Quickly remove the flower head. Place briefly on a paper towel to absorb oil. Serve at once with single/whipped double cream, demerara sugar and early strawberries with more cream or crème fraiche – finely chopped spearmint can also be added to taste.

Hawthorn Shoot Salad *Cratageus monogyna*
(May Tree, Bread and Cheese)

Young hawthorn shoots can be picked either as a cluster of young flowers with two or three leaves (known as bread and cheese) or as the elongated purple-green shoots of young leaves. Of these, the former can be added to beef or cheese sandwiches – the young flowers are rich in nectar and can have a slightly sweet flour-like taste. Alternatively, the purple-coloured shoots can be added to spring salads. They have a pleasant nutty flavour. If you have the time and patience, the scent of the flowers and petals can be extracted by simmering them in cream as a base for custard or ice cream, or using them to make a panna cotta – see the recipe for gorse flowers in March (p.71) for ingredients and method.

Jack by the Hedge Panna Cotta *Allaria petiolata*
(Hedge Garlic, Garlic Mustard)

Ingredients
6–8 large young leaves (ideally picked before flowers
have broken bud, when the flavour is best)
300ml double cream
3 leaves of gelatine
300ml semi-skimmed natural milk
A pinch of salt

Method
Wash and finely chop the fresh leaves. Pour double cream into a saucepan and bring slowly to the boil over a low heat. Leave boiling quietly until you have reduced the cream by approximately one sixth, to about 250ml. Add chopped leaves and continue to boil gently for another hour. Remove pan from heat and leave the mixture to infuse for three hours. Soak the gelatine strips in cold water. Heat the milk in a small pan. Squeeze water out of the gelatine strips and place them in the pan of milk. Stir until dissolved. Pour the infused cream through a fine sieve to strain out the leaves and then add to the milk and dissolved gelatine. Pour the panna cotta into moulds and leave in a fridge to set. Serve with fresh leaf salad and seasoning. This is a lovely recipe – the panna cotta has a refreshing, slightly mustardy/nutty tang to it.

Nettle Tip Sauce *Urtica dioica* (Stinger)

Ingredients
Approx. 35 nettle tips
12g salted butter
1 tablespoon of olive oil
1 tablespoon of coarse ground black pepper
½ pint double cream
¼ teaspoon of ground nutmeg or ½ teaspoon of ground
dried coriander

Method
The best way to pick nettle tips is between forefinger and thumb. Use Jamie Oliver's asparagus rule: pinch the top two pairs of leaves firmly between your fingers and bend the stalk, pulling gently. Where it snaps is the point at which the stem starts to become fibrous. The growing tip left in your hand will be deliciously tender. (If you are a purist, no gloves are needed to pick nettles – sometimes they hardly sting at all.) Wash the nettle tips in cold water. Bring 1½ litres of water to the boil in a saucepan. When boiling hard, drop the nettle tips in and stir with a wooden spoon. Leave boiling for about four minutes. Remove from heat and carefully pour off hot water and strain off the remainder by emptying the nettles into a colander in a sink. Press out remaining water with a wooden spoon. While still hot, place the nettles in a blender. Add the other ingredients and blend. Vary proportions to taste. This recipe is based on one for spinach that I once tried near Barcelona. Blended with nutmeg, the nettle sauce goes very well with beef.

Wild Hop Shoot Pesto *Humulus lupulus*
(Poor Man's Asparagus)

Ingredients
Approximately 25 wild hop tips (200g)
A handful of pine kernels
100g of freshly grated Parmesan cheese
2 cloves of finely chopped garlic
½ a lemon
½ teaspoon of sea salt
½ teaspoon of Sarawak black pepper
150ml olive oil.

Method
To pick wild hop shoots, use the same rule as for nettle tips. (Always check your identification. Hop leaves look like vine leaves. The climbing stems are ridged and slightly hairy or rough to touch.) After washing them, chop the hop tips into two to three inch lengths. Pour about one litre of water into a saucepan and bring to the boil. When boiling hard, drop the tips in. Leave them in the boiling water for about three minutes and then remove the pan from the heat. Carefully pour off the hot water and strain the tips. They should be nicely blanched, but still green and firm in texture. As they cool, chop the tips into smaller 5mm lengths. Heat the pine kernels in a pan with a tablespoon of olive oil until they are just about to brown. Remove the kernels from the heat and pan. Mix with the chopped garlic, salt and pepper. Pulse blend in a blender. Add the hop shoots and the remaining olive oil. Repeat the blending. Serve fresh with pasta or place the mix in a jar or pot and store in the fridge for later use.

Appendix IV:
Civil Sue and Sunkets

Jason Gathorne-Hardy

(with thanks to A O D Claxton)

Our relationships to food, work, people and the land are all intimately expressed through the language that we use in our daily lives. The garden at Glemham House has been in continuous use for almost two centuries. During this time many of these relationships have undergone huge changes, leading to an inevitable loss and change of vocabulary. In his book *The Suffolk Dialect*, A O D Claxton starts with the following quotation:

"I think it will become those of us who have a more hearty love for what is our own, than wanton longings after what is others, to fetch back some of our own words that have been jostled out in the wrong, that worse from elsewhere might be hoisted in; or else to call in from the fields and waters, shops and workhousen, that well-fraught world of words that answers works, by which all learners are taught to do and not to make a clatter."

From Fairfax's *Bulk and Selvedge of the World* (1674)

In the spirit of this excerpt, it seems appropriate to "fetch back" some of the local Suffolk dialect that would have been in common parlance during the 19th and early 20th centuries in the walled garden at Glemham House and in the local landscape – echoes of which seem still to resound around the walls, sheds and greenhouses. I have used Claxton's book as the principal source for the words that follow.

Airy wiggle ~ earwig

All manner o'what ~ all kinds of things

Arsey varsey ~ upside down

Bang ~ cheese made from skimmed milk, sometimes known as "Suffolk Thump". (The Suffolk poet Robert Bloomfield, describing Suffolk cheese, wrote that it "*..mocks the efforts of the bending blade; Or in the hog's trough rests in perfect spite, Too big to swallow, too hard to bite..*")

Bishop barnabee ~ ladybird

Battlings ~ loppings off trees used as firewood

Betsy Jane ~ a small piece of cheese on a small piece of bread

Bone in your leg ~ an affliction of people who are healthy, but persistently complain about their well being. (This phrase was still in use when I was a child

– I think I suffered from it several times – usually on winter mornings before school. Left unattended, *a bone in your leg* can develop into the much more serious condition of *mullygrubs*)

Bread and cheese ~ the first green shoots and blossom of hawthorn

Bullfice ~ puffball

Cagmag ~ to gossip

Canch ~ a slice cut from an old fashioned haystack or muck heap; a narrow strip of land

Chaits ~ scraps of leftovers from a meal fed to chickens or pigs

Charley ~ a toad

Chice ~ a morsel or taste of food

Chick ~ to germinate

Civil Sue ~ the water in which a suet pudding was boiled, used as a gravy

Criss cross row ~ the alphabet. (This reminds me of learning the alphabet and writing at Framlingham Primary School in the mid 1970s, which involved writing line after line of individual letters and words)

Dimsy day ~ a dull day

Dodman or *hodmedod* ~ snail

Dow-fulfer ~ fieldfare

Eggs and bacon ~ young shoots of wild dog rose, eaten raw

Feetings ~ footprints of animals in snow

Fisherate ~ to attend to household duties

Fletches ~ young pods of peas

Fog nightingale ~ a frog (this is one of my favourite Suffolk words)

Froize ~ a pancake

Gattikin ~ clumsy

Golt ~ heavy clay

Half arter eights/Lijahs ~ men's gaiters or leg straps, worn below the knee

Hand o'pork ~ shoulder of pork with blade bone removed

Hareweed ~ cleavers/goosegrass

Hin's nose full ~ a very small quantity

Home done ~ a joint of meat cooked right to the middle

Honky donks ~ hob-nailed boots

Horkey ~ the Harvest Home supper

Isaac and ash ~ a scythe

Jacobites ~ thistles

Jasper ~ wasp

Kichel ~ a flat Christmas cake

King Henry ~ goldfinch

Lard ~ to sweat profusely from working hard

Links ~ sausages

Lowans ~ an allowance for beer/ale in a bill

Mavis ~ thrush

Meece, mizzen ~ mice

Million ~ pumpkin

Minifer/mousehunt ~ weasel

Mowles ~ earth in good heart/good tilth

Muckinja ~ pocket handkerchief

Munjin ~ a feast or good feed

Nancy ~ a small lobster

Nettus/neat-house ~ cow barn

Nigh nor by ~ nearby

On the drag ~ running behind-hand or late

On the huh ~ on the slant or wobbled

Open his mouth ~ to ask a silly or unreasonable price for livestock or goods

Perry wind ~ a sudden whirling wind

Phoebe ~ the sun

Pikle/pickerel ~ a small piece of enclosed land, for chickens or domestic use

Pittle bed ~ dandelion (known as *Pis-en-lit* in France)

Pullen ~ poultry

Rafe hook ~ sickle

Reave ~ fresh manure

Ringe ~ row of plants in a garden, or the furrow

Risps ~ stalks of climbing plants such as peas or beans

Rudle ~ a drink made with warm beer, gin, sugar and lemon peel

Sase ~ a layer of flint in chalk

Scuppit ~ a shovel

Smur/smither/dinje ~ to drizzle or rain softly

Snotty gobbles ~ yew berries (the flesh of the fruit around the poisonous seed is remarkably sticky, causing birds to wipe it from their beaks)

Spirket ~ wooden peg upon which to hang horse harness, coats etc

Sturrens ~ small household jobs or chores

Sukey ~ kettle

Sunkets ~ delicacies, fancy cakes (eg for afternoon tea or dinner)

Swale ~ small valley

Tater trap ~ mouth

Thumb piece ~ food eaten from the hand, e.g. bread and cheese or jam

Timber hill ~ staircase leading up to bedrooms

Triculate ~ to smarten up/dress up

Wadmal ~ duffle coat

Wet bird ~ green woodpecker

Wittles ~ food/victuals

Weather head ~ a second rainbow

Weather breeder ~ a particularly fine day in the middle of a run of bad weather, taken as a sign that worse is to come

Watering ~ a ford

Wobble ~ to wrap up warmly

Wonmil ~ a soft cheese made from unskimmed milk. (The Reeve family in the village of Friston were making a soft cheese called *Buxlow Wonmil* up until 2010, alongside a harder cheese called *Buxlow Paigle*. Both were full of flavour and are much missed)

When last comes last ~ the end/finally

Yow-a-munchy ~ you amongst yourselves

One of the few places where a smattering of Suffolk dialect can still be heard is Campsea Ashe Market, held every Monday at Abbotts Auction Rooms at Campsea Ashe, near Wickham Market. Up until the late 1990s it was one of the weekly livestock markets that rotated around the Alde Valley (Framlingham was on Tuesdays, Saxmundham on Wednesdays). Today the livestock are long gone, but the "deadstock" remains – the traditional name for house clearance items and old farm and garden implements. During the winter months, between October and February, the Auction Rooms also host a weekly sale of poultry and game. Partridges, ducks, woodcock, geese, pigeons, pheasant, rabbits and the occasional hare from surrounding farms are all auctioned off after a punctual ten o'clock start. The climax is the annual Christmas Poultry Sale, at which hundreds of plucked and dressed turkeys[*], geese, chickens, guinea fowl and capons are sold to the highest bidder. A steamy tea room serving home made sausage rolls, cheese scones and cakes with tea or milky coffee rounds off a visit to the market for many. The food and drinks taste especially good on the dullest, wettest winter Mondays, when the windows are draped with condensation and the air is thick with the conversation of friends and acquaintances catching up.

[*] If you leave a bid at the Christmas Poultry Sale, one word of warning. A "gobbler" is a live turkey. My mother learned this the hard way in the 1970s. She left a bid with a steward for Christmas turkeys. He asked if gobblers would be all right. She said that she thought that gobblers would be fine. Later in the day we drove to the market and found two very large, proud Norfolk black turkeys waiting for us. They just about fitted in the back of our Ford Cortina estate and, gobbling in alarm, lived loudly up to their name. By the time we got home, barely five miles away, the birds had become family friends. I think an emergency order was placed with Revetts butcher in Wickham Market.

Bibliography:

Jason Gathorne-Hardy

The following books were consulted in the writing of this book. Those marked with a star (*) include direct references to the Upper Alde Valley and Great Glemham. The works of George Crabbe, H W Freeman, George Ewart Evans, Ronald Blythe, Julian Tennyson and Hugh Barrett represent a vein of literature that seems particular to the landscape of the Alde Valley and East Suffolk, as distinctive as the sandwiched layers of clay, loams, sand and alluvial soils that run through it. The recipe books are from the shelves of my own and my parents' kitchens – my shelves are much shorter and smaller than theirs. The Aldeburgh Music Festival programmes that I explored as reference material all belonged to my dear grandmother, Fidelity Cranbrook. In reading them I realised that all the things that this book seeks to celebrate – the coming together of food, gardening, landscape and the arts – are ageless. They are to be found in the Festival programmes from the 1950s and 1970s.

*Aldeburgh Festival of Music and the Arts. Festival programmes for 1958, 1973, 1975

Arnott, W G *Alde Estuary – The Story of a Suffolk River* 1952, Norman Adlard & Co Ltd, Ipswich

Bareham, Terence *George Crabbe* 1977, Vision Press Ltd, London

*Barrett, Hugh *A Good Living* 2002, Old Pond Publishing, Ipswich

Batey, Mavis *Regency Gardens* 1995, Shire Garden Series, Shire Publications, Princes Risborough

Bird, Richard and Houdret, Jessica *Kitchen and Herb Gardener* 2000, Lorenz Books, Anness Publishing Ltd, London

*Blythe, Ronald. *Akenfield: Portrait of an English Village*. First published in 1969 by Allen Lane. 2005, Penguin Classics, London. (The Magistrate was based on Fidelity Cranbrook and The Ploughman was Tony Heffer, who worked at Great Glemham Farms for 53 years, receiving his long service award from the Suffolk Agricultural Association in 2010.)

Carluccio, Antonio. *Antonio Carluccio Goes Wild* 2001, Headline Book Publishing, Hodder Headline, London

Claxton, A. O. D. *The Suffolk Dialect of the Twentieth Century* 1968, Norman Adlard and Co, Ipswich

Clevely, Andy; Mackley, Lesley; Morris, Sallie; Richmond, Katherine *Cooking with Herbs and Spices* 2004, Anness Publishing Ltd, London

*Crabbe, George (junior) *The Poetical Works of the Rev George Crabbe with his Letters and Journals, and his Life, by his Son* 1834, John Murray, Albemarle Street, London. Printed in eight volumes

*Cranbrook, 4th Earl of (John David Gathorne-Hardy) *Parnassian Molehill an Anthology of Suffolk Verse 1327-1864* 1953 Cowell, Ipswich. 2001 new edition with introduction by Ronald Blythe. Aldeburgh Bookshop

* Cranbrook, 5th Earl of (Gathorne Gathorne-Hardy) *In Good Hands – The Endurance of a Regency Park and Garden at Glemham House, Great Glemham* 2009-10. Unpublished manuscript

David, Elizabeth *Mediterranean Food* 1958. Faber & Faber Ltd, London

Edwards, Russell *The Suffolk Coast* 1991, Terence Dalton Ltd, Lavenham, Suffolk

Ewart Evans, George *Ask the Fellows Who Cut the Hay* 1956, Faber & Faber. 2010, Full Circle Editions

Ewart Evans, George *The Crooked Scythe* 1993, Faber & Faber Ltd, London

Ewart Evans, George. *The Farm and the Village* 1969, Faber & Faber Ltd, London

Ewart Evans, George *The Horse in the Furrow* 1960, Faber & Faber Ltd, London

Ewart Evans, George *Spoken History* 1987, Faber & Faber Ltd, London

Fearnley-Whittingstall, Hugh *The River Cottage Meat Book* 2004, Hodder & Stoughton Ltd, London

Fincham, Paul *The Suffolk We Live in* First published 1976. 1983 edition, Barbara Hopkins Books, Woodbridge, Suffolk

*Freeman, H. W. *Joseph and His Brethren* First published 1928. 2003 edition, Old Pond Publishing, Ipswich, Suffolk

*Gishford, Anthony (Editor) *A Tribute to Benjamin Britten on his Fiftieth Birthday* 1963, Faber & Faber Ltd, London

Grieves, Guy and Miers, Thomasina *The Wild Gourmets* 2007, Bloomsbury Publishing, London

Harrison, S G; Masefield, G B; Wallis, M *The Oxford Book of Food Plants* 1969, O.U.P, Oxford

Hartley, Dorothy *Food in England* First edition 1954. Paperback edition 1999, Little, Brown & Co, London

Hix, Mark *British Regional Food* 2006, Quadrille
  Publishing Ltd, London

Jekyll, Lady Agnes Graham *Kitchen Essays* First
  published in 1922. Republished in 2001 by
  Persephone Books Ltd, London
Jobson, Allan *Portrait of Suffolk* 1973, Robert Hale
  Ltd, London

Kapsazova, Sonja *The Bulgarian National Cuisine in
  My Home* The Kapsazov's Houses, Kovachevitsa,
  Bulgaria
K'Eogh, John *An Irish Herbal : Botanalogia
  Universalis Hibernica* (1735). Republished 1986,
  Ed. Michael Scott; The Wellingborough Press,
  Northamptonshire

Mabey, Richard *Food for Free* 1972, Collins, London
Miers, Thomasina *Cook* 2006,
  HarperCollinsPublishers, London

Perrin, R. M. S. *Topography, Geology and Soils* 1972.
  In *East Anglian Forests* edited by Herbert L. Edlin;
  published for The Forestry Commission by Her
  Majesty's Stationery Office
Phillips, Roger *Wild Food* 1986, Little, Brown & Co,
  London
Phillips, Roger *Mushrooms and Other Fungi of Great
  Britain and Europe* 1981, Pan Books
Pollock, Michael *Vegetable and Fruit Gardening* 2008,
  The Royal Horticultural Society, Dorling Kindersley
  Ltd, London
*Powell, Neil *George Crabbe – An English Life 1754-
  1832* 2004, Pimlico, London

Rackham, Oliver *The History of the Countryside* J M
  Dent. 1986. Revised 1990
*Rackham, Oliver *Trees and Woodland in the British
  Landscape* J M Dent. 1976

*Scarfe, Norman *The Suffolk Landscape* 1972, Hodder
  & Stoughton, London
Simons, Arthur J. *The Vegetable Grower's Handbook,
  Volume I* 1945, Penguin Books, London/New York

Taylor Simeti, Mary *Sicilian Food* 1999, Grub Street,
  London
*Tennyson, Julian *Suffolk Scene* 1949, Blackie & Son,
  London. First published 1939

Uglow, Jenny *A Little History of British Gardening*
  2004, Chatto & Windus, London

Wake-Walker, Jenny *Time & Concord – Aldeburgh
  Festival Recollections* 1997, Autograph Books,
  Saxmundham
*Williamson, Tom *Suffolk's Gardens and Parks* 2000
  *Designed Landscapes from the Tudors to the
  Victorians* Windgather Press

Acknowledgements

I dedicate this book to my family and friends, in Britain and Malaysia. Special thanks also go to family and fellow Food Adventurers who have contributed to this book including Marcia Blakeham, Sukie Hemming and Natalia Wilkinson; and to the following professional chefs and cooks:

Andrew Blackburn, former chef owner of the Bell Hotel, Saxmundham
(a.spinney@btinternet.com)
Stephanie Bullard, who works as a private cook
Peter Clark, head chef at Café 1885 in Snape Maltings (www.snapemaltings.co.uk)
Claire Bruce-Clayton, co-owner of award winning Lawsons Delicatessen in
Aldeburgh (www.lawsonsdelicatessen.co.uk)
Miche Fabre Lewin, artist cuisiniere from Oxfordshire
Flora Gathorne-Hardy, geographer, artist and landscape designer through Topio
(www.topio.co.uk), also collaborating on food/art projects with Miche Fabre Lewin
David Grimwood, owner and chef of Froize Inn at Chillesford in East Suffolk
(www.froize.co.uk)
Peter Harrison, who works privately and as a cook with Lawsons Delicatessen
(www.lawsonsdelicatessen.co.uk)
William and Miranda Kendal, who own and manage Maple Farm near Saxmundham
(www.maplefarmkelsale.co.uk)
Gerard King, head butcher and manager of award winning Broxted Butchery at The
Suffolk Food Hall in Wherstead near Ipswich (www.suffolkfoodhall.co.uk)
Lola de Mille, who runs a catering company in Norwich (De Mille's on Wheels –
07763126143)
Rob Sledmere, who helped with research, creator of The Suffolk Providore Ltd
(www.thesuffolkprovidore.co.uk)

Tessa Newcomb would like to thank Gathorne and Caroline Cranbrook, the
Gathorne-Hardy family, the gardeners at Glemham House and Full Circle Editions

All paintings and drawings by Tessa Newcomb
Endpapers *Aerial View of the Walled Garden* drawn by Jason Gathorne-Hardy © 2012
Photographic credits:
Kate Eshelby: p.26, p.30, p.35
Tessa's paintings and drawings photographed by John Christie
Archive photographs © The Earl and Countess of Cranbrook, Jason Gathorne-
Hardy, Simon and Harriet Frazer and Judy Waters

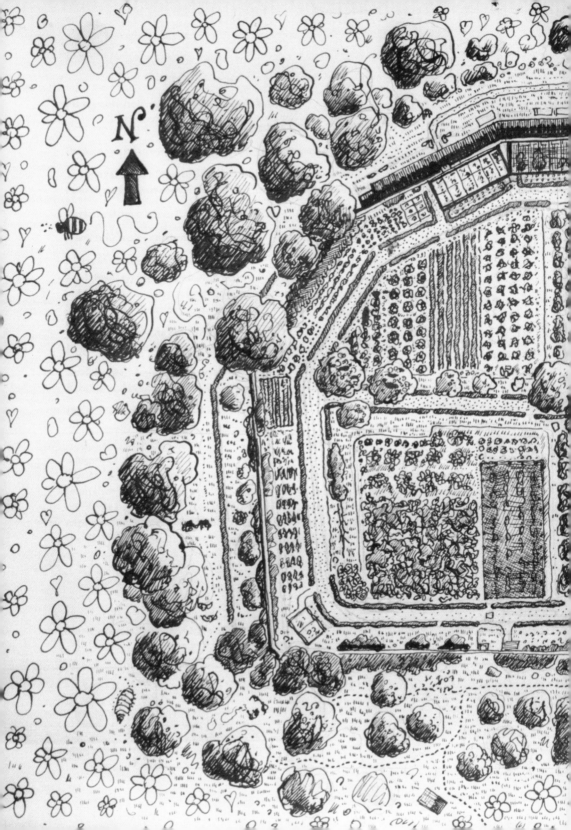